The Jews in the Works of the Church Fathers

ANALECTA GORGIANA

67

General Editor
George Anton Kiraz

Analecta Gorgiana is a collection of long essays and short monographs which are consistently cited by modern scholars but previously difficult to find because of their original appearance in obscure publications. Now conveniently published, these essays are not only vital for our understanding of the history of research and ideas, but are also indispensable tools for the continuation and development of on-going research. Carefully selected by a team of scholars based on their relevance to modern scholarship, these essays can now be fully utilized by scholars and proudly owned by libraries.

The Jews in the Works of the Church Fathers

Sources for Understanding the Agaddah

SAMUEL KRAUSS

GORGIAS PRESS
2007

First Gorgias Press Edition, 2007

The special contents of this edition are copyright © 2007 by
Gorgias Press LLC

All rights reserved under International and Pan-American Copyright Conventions. No part of this publication may be reproduced, stored in a retrieval system or transmitted in any form or by any means, electronic, mechanical, photocopying, recording, scanning or otherwise without the prior written permission of Gorgias Press LLC.

Published in the United States of America by Gorgias Press LLC, New Jersey

This edition is a facsimile reprint of the
original edition published in *The Jewish Quarterly Review* , London, 1892-4,
Vols. 5-7.

ISBN 978-1-59333-883-1

ISSN 1935-6854

GORGIAS PRESS
46 Orris Ave., Piscataway, NJ 08854 USA
www.gorgiaspress.com

The paper used in this publication meets the minimum requirements of the
American National Standards.

Printed in the United States of America

TABLE OF CONTENTS

Table of Contents v
Introduction 1
1 Justin Martyr 2
2 Clement of Alexandria 13
3 Origen 18
4 Eusebius 37
5 Ephraem Syrus 43
6 Jerome 55

THE JEWS IN THE WORKS OF THE CHURCH FATHERS.

FOR the history and science of Judaism, and especially for a full understanding of the Agada, the study of the Church Fathers undeniably possesses considerable importance. Naturally all of them are not of the same value. Those who lived in Italy, Spain, or Gaul, and had little communication with Jews, are of minor significance for Jewish literature, compared with the Fathers of Palestine, Syria, and Egypt. I shall therefore pay the most attention to those Fathers whose writings promise the richest results, and we can herein confidently follow the lead of Jerome, who, in his reply to his opponent Rufinus's charge, that he associated too much with Jews, quoted the examples of Origen, Clement, and Eusebius, none of whom disdained to receive instruction from teachers of the Hebrew race (Lib. I., adv. Ruff., c. 13, vol. ii., p. 469, Ed. Vallarsi). If the first notable Father, Justin, and Ephraem Syrus, Jerome's younger contemporary, be added, we obtain the following list of Ecclesiastics, whose writings are of especial interest to us :— Justin Martyr, Clemens Alexandrinus, Origen, Eusebius, Ephraem Syrus, and Jerome.

In the last four decades, since the importance of Patristic literature has obtained a gradually increasing recognition in Jewish circles, students have always sought in the Fathers for Agadic elements which they might collate with Hebrew sources. The fact has, however, been lost sight of, that these Agadas have not always come direct from the Jews. Many of those found in the Church literature must be regarded as the product of independent development. The Agadic exegesis of the Scriptures was peculiar to the spirit of the times, and flourished among the Christians as exuberantly as among the Jews. The accounts in the Church Fathers of Judaism and of Jewish conditions and modes of life are, in my opinion, no less worthy of regard than the Agadic elements there preserved. I shall, therefore, direct my main attention to this class of notices, and only speak of such Agadas as were expressly and explicitly borrowed from the Jews.

For the works of Justin, Clement, Origen and Eusebius, I have used Migne's *Patrologie* (M.); for Ephraem, the Roman edition (R.) of 1732-43; for Jerome, Vallarsi's edition (V.), Verona, 1734-42. Other editions will be quoted occasionally.

I.

JUSTIN MARTYR.

Justin Martyr was born about 100 A.D., in Flavia Neapolis, formerly called Sichem, in the country of the Samaritans. He terms himself a Samaritan, which does not, however, mean that he belonged to the religious sect of the Samaritans, but that they were his countrymen.[1] He, indeed, expressly states that he was one of the uncircumcised.[2] At a later period he came to Ephesus, the scene of his dialogue with the Jew, Tryphon (Eusebius *H. E.*, iv. 18); and here he zealously propagated Christianity among the Jews.[3] The date of the Dialogue coincides with the period of the revolt under Bar Cochba (132—135). That obstinate contest is frequently mentioned in it;[4] and Tryphon is described as a fugitive who escaped from the turmoil of Palestine to peaceful Ephesus.[5]

---

[1] *Dial.* c. 120 (vi. 755, M.), ... ἀπὸ τοῦ γένους τοῦ ἐμοῦ, λέγω δὲ τῶν Σαμαρέων.

[2] *Ib.* c. 29 (vi. 537, M.), τίς οὖν ἔτι μοι περιτομῆς λόγος ....

[3] This follows from several passages of the *Dialogue*; v. Wetzer-Welte's *Kirchenlexicon*, vi. 2067.

[4] *E.g. Dial.* c. 108 (vi. 725, M.), cp. *Apol.* I. 31 (vi. 376, M.).

[5] At the beginning of the *Dialogue*.

These data alone should have sufficed to prove the historical character of the Dialogue. Nevertheless, scholars have apparently favoured the theory that it is only a literary framework for presenting Justin's views, and is purely imaginary. Emphasis is laid upon the fact that Tryphon makes concessions to Justin such as no faithful Jew would possibly have made.[1] The obvious explanation is that politeness induced Tryphon to adopt a conciliatory and yielding tone. Throughout the Dialogue he appears as an enlightened Jew, imbued with Hellenistic culture, who is anxious to exhibit extreme courtesy towards his adversary. He is introduced as a man of education and a philosopher. When Justin remarks, in the course of the interview, that he has no oratorical ability, the Jew replies with tact: "You must be jesting; your conversation proves you a past master in rhetoric."[2] Tryphon's concessions are, moreover, in most cases, only hypothetical; and Justin very often imitates him in this respect, admitting even once for instance, for the sake of argument, that Jesus was nothing more than a *Magus*.[3] Besides, details are given which are unsuitable to a fictitious dialogue, but have a meaning if we assume that the writer reports events which actually took place. On the first day, we are told, no strangers were present at the interview; on the second day, however, Tryphon is joined by some Jews of Ephesus, who take a part in the discussion.[4] One of them begs that a remark which had pleased him might be repeated, and Justin complies with the request.[5] Another of those who had accompanied Tryphon on the second day, called Mnaseas, also joins in

---

[1] Weizsaecker, *Jahrb. für Theologie* XII. (1867), p. 63.

[2] *Dial.* c. 58 (vi. 606, M.), οὐ κατασκευὴν λόγων ἐν μόνῃ τέχνῃ ἐπιδείκνυσθαι σπεύδω.... Καὶ ὁ Τρύφων· εἰρωνεύεσθαι δέ μοι δοκεῖς, λέγων δύναμιν λόγων τεχνικῶν μὴ κεκτῆσθαι.

[3] *Apol.* I. c. 30 (vi. 273, M.).

[4] *Dial.* c. 118. (vi. 749, M.), διὰ τοὺς σήμερον σὺν σοὶ ἀφιγμένους....

[5] *Ib.* c. 74 (vi. 649, M.).

the debate.[1] This circumstance suggests the inference that not only Tryphon, who from the first inspired Justin with respect as a man of Hellenic culture, but that other members of the Jewish community of Ephesus were also sufficiently well educated to be able to stand their ground against the learned Church Father. Occasionally they give audible token of their satisfaction or disapproval,[2] even applauding and hissing, just as in a theatre.[3] Justin repeatedly, in the course of the disputation, bears testimony to the respect he feels for his learned opponent, and promises, when the Dialogue appears in its written form, to truthfully present Tryphon's views.[4] At the close of the debate, Jew and Christian confess that they have learnt much from one another, and part with expressions of mutual goodwill.[5] These details can only be reminiscences of a real event.

That Tryphon was the famous sage Tarphon (טרפון) is more justly discredited. Justin's description of his antagonist does not tally with what we know of R. Tarphon. The Tanaite was certainly not a philosopher of Tryphon's type. Though Tarphon and Tryphon are not identical, Graetz thinks the name was purposely chosen by the Father, so that he might be able to boast that he had won over the eminent teacher, Tarphon, to Christianity.[6] But it is questionable whether the Hebrew טרפון really cor-

---

[1] Ib. c. 85 (vi. 677, M.), οὗ καὶ πάλιν ἐπιμνησθήσομαι διὰ τούτου, τοὺς μὴ καὶ χθὲς σύνοντας ἡμῖν.... Καὶ Μνασέας δέ τις ὀνόματι τῶν συνελθόντων αὐτοῖς τῇ δευτέρᾳ ἡμέρᾳ εἶπε....

[2] Ib. c. 38 (vi. 557, M.), μὴ ταράσσεσθε δέ, ἀλλὰ μᾶλλον προθυμότεροι γενόμενοι ἀκροαταὶ καὶ ἐξετασταὶ μένετε καταφρονοῦντες τῆς παραδόσεως τῶν ὑμετέρων διδασκάλων.

[3] Ib. c. 122 (vi. 760, M.), καὶ ὥσπερ ἐν θεάτρῳ ἀνέκραγόν τινες τῶν τῇ δευτέρᾳ ἀφιγμένων.

[4] Ib. c. 80 (vi. 664. M.), τῶν γεγενημένων ἡμῖν λόγων ἁπάντων.... σύνταξιν ποιήσομαι ἐν οἷς καὶ τοῦτο ὁμολογοῦντά με ὃ καὶ πρὸς ὑμᾶς ὁμολογῶ, ἐγγράψω.

[5] Ib. ad fin.

[6] Gnosticismus u. Judenth., p. 17.

responds to the Greek Τρύφων, in which case only could Justin have intended טרפון by his Τρύφων. Jerome, in his list of the oldest Tanaim, calls טרפון 'ר Telphon.[1] He would have probably written Τρύφων had the two names been equivalent.[2] Goldfahn's theory that Tryphon was selected by Justin, because it sounded like δρύπτω, needs no refutation.[3]

Accepting the historical character of the Dialogue, we naturally cannot seek for covert allusions in the name Tryphon. It was probably in common use among the Jews of that age, and there is nothing remarkable in the fact of Justin's having happened to meet a Jew with this name. The same is the case with Mnaseas, which was also frequent from an early period. We find it in Josephus (*Cont. Apion*. i. 23). שמעון בן מנסיא 'ר, of a subsequent date, is frequently mentioned in Mishna, Tosefta, Talmud and Midrash; in T. Babli (Beza 30*b*) the name is spelt מנשיא. Zunz quotes a Mnasea, grandson of a Mnasea, from the Seder-ha-doroth, fol. 68*b* (Gesammelte Schriften II., p. 23). Tryphon and Mnasea were thus ordinary names among the Jews; and nothing is less surprising than that Justin's chief opponent in the Dialogue, and another Jew of Ephesus, should have borne them.

Justin's writings constitute the first attempt which has come down to us to justify Christianity before the bar of the ancient religious powers, Heathenism and Judaism. Early Christendom still clung somewhat nervously to the old faith. Christians still practised many Jewish customs,[4] and Justin feels the need of offering an excuse for the

---

[1] In Is. viii. 11.

[2] A. Geiger, *Jüd. Zeitschrift* v. 173, proposes to read instead of Delphon (a variant of Telphon) simply *Tarphon*; this is surely inadmissible; טרפון is perhaps the same as Τερπών (Fick, *Griech. Personennamen*, p. 81), which corresponds more closely to the form Telphon.

[3] Goldfahn, *Justin Martyr und die Agada* in Graetz's *Monatsschrift* XXII. (1873), p. 49, *et seq.*

[4] Smith-Wace, *Dict. of Christian Biography*, III. 581.

Christian transference of the Sabbath-day to Sunday.[1] Judaism has no right, the Father thinks, to thrust out its daughter Christianity, for it has also produced other heresies which it does not disown. The Sadducees, Genistae, Meristae, Galilaei, Helleniani, Pharisaei and Baptistae are all Jewish sects, so that it becomes a matter of some difficulty to decide which among them represents the real Judaism.[2] To this argument Justin attaches special importance, deeming it expedient at the same time to apologise to the Jews for the harshness of his words.[3] The Jews, he urges, had sent emissaries in all directions to calumniate the new sect.[4] This charge recurs in almost every Church Father; it is also frequently asserted that the Hebrews were zealously engaged in proselytizing. Thus in Justin's time, we may conclude with a high degree of probability, Judaism still retained its power of expansion. The prophetic promise that the Word of God would reach distant nations the Hebrews saw fulfilled in the accession of proselytes to their ranks, the Christians, in the spread of their own creed.[5]

---

[1] *Dial.* c. 24 (vi. 528, M.).

[2] The names of these sects are cited by Eusebius, *H. E.* iv. 22 (xx. 381, M.), from the work of an older author, Hegesippus. There they are called Ἐσσαῖοι, Γαλιλαῖοι, Ἡμεροβάπτισται, Μασβοθαῖοι, Σαμαρεῖται, Σαδδουκαῖοι, Φαρισσαῖοι. In the *Indiculum Haereseon*, which is ascribed to Jerome, the *Hemerobaptistae, qui quotidie corpora sua et domum et supellectilem lavant* figure as the tenth sect. We recognise this sect as the טובלי שחרית of *Berach*, III. 6c; they must not be confused with the Essenes. Justin's Baptistae are very likely the same as these Hemerobaptistae. Concerning the Genistae, Meristae, Galilaei and Helleneiani the views of scholars are widely divergent, and we will leave the question open. It is remarkable, however, that the *Essaeans* are mentioned neither by Justin nor by Eusebius, and not even by Isodorus, *Orig. libr.* VIII.; the Christians probably felt that they themselves had taken their origin from this sect, and were, therefore, unwilling to designate them as heretics.

[3] *Dial.* c. 80 (vi. 665, M.), καὶ μὴ ἀηδῶς ἀκούσητέ μου πάντα ἃ φρονῶ λέγοντος. [4] *Ib.* c. 108 (vi. 725, M.).

[5] *Ib.* c. 122 (vi. 760, M.), concerning Is. xlix. 6, ταῦτα ὑμεῖς μὲν εἰς τὸν Γηόραν καὶ τοὺς προσηλύτους εἰρῆσθαι νομίζετε.—Γηόρα is either גרים or גולה.

Jewish religious teachers are frequently mentioned by Justin, usually under the title of Rabbi,[1] sometimes also simply as διδάσκαλοι;[2] in a few instances, as heads of the Synagogue, ἀρχισυνάγωγοι;[3] an insulting epithet is invariably added. The Rabbinical teachings are termed traditions, παραδόσεις.[4] Instruction was given at the conclusion of divine worship.[5] Disputations between learned Christians and Jewish Rabbis were the order of the day. Numerous specimens are found in Hebrew literature. Justin ridicules the tactics of the Jewish controversialists, who always hunted up their opponents' weak points, like the fly which settles on sore places. If, at a disputation, a multitude of well-considered and well-weighed arguments are adduced, the Jews will always discover a neglected point open to attack.[6] Such controversies might sometimes prove disadvantageous to Judaism, where expert Christian dialecticians overwhelmed ignorant Jews with arguments which they were not prepared to answer, and by which they would have to acknowledge themselves beaten. Justin strove personally for the conversion of the Jews; his efforts were, however, futile, owing to the accident that he met his match in his opponents at Ephesus. Ordinary Jews, not specially skilled in controversy, were strictly enjoined to avoid polemics with Christians.[7] And even Tryphon, who presented so bold a front to his opponent, regretted his breach of this rule.[8] By this we

---

[1] *Dial* c. 112 (vi. 736, M.), Θελόντων 'Ραββί, 'Ραββί καλεῖσθαι.
[2] *Ib.* c. 110 (vi. 729, M.), *et passim.*   [3] *Ib.* c. 137 (vi. 792, M.).
[4] *Ib.* c. 38 (vi. 557, M.), *et passim.*
[5] *Ib.* c. 137 (vi. 792, M.), διδάσκουσιν .... μετὰ τὴν προσευχήν.
[6] *Ib.* c. 115 (vi. 744, M.), "Ὥσπερ γὰρ αἱ μυῖαι ἐπὶ τὰ ἕλκη προστρέχετε καὶ ἐφίπτασθε. κἂν γὰρ μυρία τις εἴπῃ καλῶς, ἓν δὲ σμικρὸν ὁτιοῦν εἴπῃ μὴ εὐάρεστον ὑμῖν, ἢ μὴ νοούμενον ἢ μὴ πρὸς τὸ ἀκριβές, τῶν μὲν πολλῶν καλῶν οὐ πεφροντίκατε, τοῦ δὲ μικροῦ ῥηματίου ἐπιλαμβάνεσθε, καὶ κατασκευάζειν αὐτὸ ὡς ἀσέβημα καὶ ἀδίκημα σπουδάζετε.
[7] *Ib.* c. 112 (vi. 736, M.), ἡ καὶ ἡμῶν ἐξηγουμένων παραγγέλλουσιν ὑμῖν μηδὲ ὅλως ἐπαίειν, μηδὲ εἰς κοινωνίαν λόγων ἐλθεῖν.
[8] *Ib.* c. 38 (vi. 556, M.), καὶ ὁ Τρύφων εἶπεν .... καλὸν ἦν πεισθέντας ἡμᾶς τοῖς διδασκάλοις νομοθετήσασι μηδενὶ ἐξ ὑμῶν ὁμιλεῖν ....

may gather how the Rabbinic regulations were respected by the people at large. A Jew of Ephesus tells us that for the solution of his doubts and difficulties he often referred to the Rabbis, whom the people regarded as their appointed leaders.[1]

The differences between the Synagogue and the Church turn mostly on the exegesis of Holy Writ; a large portion of the Agada in the Midrash and Talmud is a polemic against Christianity. The text of the Scriptures also constituted an important subject of controversy; the Christians usually read into the Bible more than it contained. Moreover, instead of admitting that their copies were often incorrect, they cherished the delusion that the Jews had falsified and mutilated the text for polemical purposes. This charge already occurs in Justin, who accuses the Jews of altering παρθένος in Is. vii. 14 into νεᾶνις, in order to nullify a Christological argument.[2] He quotes many passages which, he alleges, are only to be found in the old texts, but have been omitted from the new editions.[3] But he is honest enough to reject a manifest Christological gloss interpolated in the Greek version, and gives the preference in this case to the Hebrew text.[4]

In Justin we also meet with a charge which, as far as we know, does not recur in any other Church Father. He accuses the Rabbis of encouraging immorality by sanctioning polygamy among their co-religionists, and

---

[1] *Ib.* c. 94 (vi. 701, M.).   [2] *Ib.* c. 68 (vi. 633, M.).

[3] *Ib.* c. 72 (vi. 645), on Jerem. xi. 19, καὶ ἐπειδὴ ἡ περικοπὴ ἡ ἐκ τῶν λόγων τοῦ 'Ιερεμίου ἔτι ἐστὶν ἐγγεγραμμένη ἔν τισιν ἀντιγράφοις τῶν ἐν συναγωγαῖς 'Ιουδαίων· πρὸ γὰρ ὀλίγου χρόνου ταῦτα ἐξέκοψαν. He cites similar passages to the same effect.

[4] This gloss is the notorious ἀπὸ τοῦ ξύλου which was said to be the reading in Ps. xcvi. (xcv.). Besides occurring in Justin, *Dial.* c. 73 (vi 645, M.), this interpolation is found only in Latin Fathers, such as Tertullian, Ambrosius, Augustinus, Leo and Gregorius Magnus, who manage to talk a great deal of nonsense concerning the "a ligno."

permitting them to lust after fair women.[1] He blames the facility with which marriages are contracted. When a Jew is abroad, the first thing he does is to take another wife.[2] This matrimonial liberty was indeed, as a matter of fact, a painful characteristic of Talmudic times.

Justin, too, is the first who imputes to the Jews the crime of mocking at and insulting Jesus. This accusation was fraught with terrible consequences for them. It is repeated by all the Fathers of the first four centuries, and though the accounts have been frequently examined, the precise character and truth of this charge have never yet been definitely established. I take the liberty, therefore, of discussing this branch of our subject in some detail.

Although the Fathers are clear as to the fact of a curse pronounced by the Jews, they differ widely as to the object of the curse. Some assert that Jesus was cursed; others that the malediction was directed against Christianity or the Christians. Starting from this point of difference, we classify the weightier statements bearing on this subject under three heads.

I. Malediction against Jesus. Justin, *Dialogue*, c. 103 (vi. 720, M.), (cp. vi. 553, M.), καὶ μάλιστα τοὺς ἐν ταῖς συναγωγαῖς, καταναθεματίσαντας καὶ καταναθεματίζοντας ἐπ' αὐτὸν τοῦτον τὸν Χριστὸν; Origen, *Hom. in Jerem.* xviii. 12 (xiii. 487, M.), Εἴσελθε εἰς τὰς τῶν Ἰουδαίων συναγωγάς, καὶ ἴδε τὸν Ἰησοῦν καθ' ἡμέραν ὑπ' αὐτῶν τῇ γλώσσῃ τῆς βλασφημίας μαστιγούμενον.

II. Against Christians and Christianity. Justin, *Dialogue*, c. 16 (vi. 512, M.), καταρώμενοι ἐν ταῖς συναγωγαῖς ὑμῶν τοὺς πιστεύοντας ἐπὶ τὸν Χριστὸν. Similarly *ib.* c.

---

[1] *Dial.* c. 134 (vi. 785, M.), τοῖς ἀσυνέτοις καὶ τυφλοῖς διδασκάλοις ὑμῶν, οἵτινες καὶ μέχρι νῦν καὶ τέσσαρας καὶ πέντε ἔχειν ὑμᾶς ἕκαστον συγχωροῦσι καὶ ἐὰν εὔμορφόν τις ἰδὼν ἐπιθυμήσῃ αὐτῆς.

[2] *Ib.* c. 141 (vi. 800, M.), καὶ ὅσας βούλεται λαμβάνειν γυναῖκας, ὁποῖον πράττουσιν οἱ ἀπὸ τοῦ γένους ὑμῶν ἄνθρωποι, κατὰ πᾶσαν γῆν, ἔνθα ἂν ἐπιδημήσωσιν ἢ προσπεμφθῶσιν, ἀγόμενοι ὀνόματι γάμου γυναῖκας.

93, (vi. 700, M.)[1]; Origen, *Hom. in Jerem.* xviii. 12 (xiii. 485, M.), καὶ μέχρι νῦν, ὑπὸ παρανόμου ἀρχιερέως λόγου προστάσσομενοι Ἐβιωναῖοι[2] τύπτουσι τὸν Ἀπόστολον Ἰησοῦ Χριστοῦ λόγοις δυσφήμοις.

III. Against the Nazarenes. Epiphanius, *Haeres.*, xxix. 9, Πάνυ δὲ οὗτοι ἐχθροὶ τοῖς Ἰουδαίοις ὑπάρχουσιν. Οὐ μόνον γὰρ οἱ τῶν Ἰουδαίων παῖδες πρὸς τούτους κέκτηνται μῖσος, ἀλ ἀνιστάμενοι ἔσωθεν (*l.* ἕωθεν) καὶ μέσης ἡμέρας καὶ περὶ τὴν ἑσπέραν, τρὶς τῆς ἡμέρας, ὅτε τὰς εὐχὰς ἐπιτελοῦσιν ἐν ταῖς αὐτῶν συναγωγαῖς, ἐπαρῶνται αὐτοῖς καὶ ἀναθεματίζουσι φάσκοντες, ὅτι ἐπικαταράσαι ὁ Θεὸς τοὺς Ναζωραίους. Jerome in Isaiah ii. 18, Sub nomine Nazaræorum anathematizant vocabulum Christianum. *Ib.* 49, 7, Christo sub nomine Nazaræorum maledicunt. *Ib.* 52, 4, sub nomine, ut saepe dixi, Nazaræorum ter die in Christianos congerunt maledicta, etc., etc.

This last group is in various ways most instructive. We learn from it that the curse was pronounced thrice daily; the eighteen Benedictions are obviously suggested. Epiphanius has further the important notice that it was recited ὅτε τὰς εὐχὰς ἐπιτελοῦσιν, which does not mean "at the conclusion of the prayers,"[3] but "while they read the prayers." The commination was thus a portion of the daily service, and has long since been justly identified with the ברכת המינים, "the prayer against heretics." That this blessing differed in Talmudic times from its present form is quite clear. It must then have explicitly named the Nazarenes, for Epiphanius gives us the definite formula, "May God curse the Nazarenes." The Talmud, which fully discusses this "blessing," nowhere hints that the Nazarenes

---

[1] On this v. Goldfahn, *ibid*, p. 56.

[2] The Ebionites, as is the case in many other respects, are here placed on a level with the Jews; what is predicated about them applies also to the Jews.

[3] This is Schuerer's opinion: *Geschichte des jüd. Volkes im Zeitalter Jesu Christi*, II. 387. The passage of Justin adduced there is not exactly in place.

figured in it. Indeed, although several Christian sects are named in that extensive literature, the Nazarenes do not once occur in it.¹ This by no means proves that this name was unknown to the Talmudic doctors. Probably נוצרי very often occurred in the Talmud, but has been erased by the mediæval censors. There were sufficient grounds for this. Catholic Christendom hated other Christian heresies as much as Judaism did, and therefore tolerated allusions to them in the Talmud. But it would not permit mention of the Nazarenes, for these, at an earlier period, were synonymous with the Christians. The Christians were called Nazarenes,² a name which they have retained in Jewish literature to this day. Our quotation from Jerome now becomes clear: *The Jews curse the Christians or Christ under the name of Nazarenes, i.e.*, the malediction in the liturgy is nominally directed against the Nazarenes but really against the Christians. From the turn of the phrase, it is evident that Jerome thought he had made a discovery. "How artful the Jews are," he seems to say, "they curse the Nazarenes when they mean the Christians." This then is established, that the so-called Benediction of the Minim contained, in ancient times, the term נוצרי; and, in fact, a gloss of Rashi, which escaped the censors, and is still preserved in later authorities, makes it clear that, in his days even, the Blessing still retained the term נוצרי.³

The problem still remains, Which expression is it that has replaced the original נוצרי? What word has been substituted for it by the censors or out of fear of them? J. Derenbourg assumes that the original form of the Benediction consisted of the following three parts: ולמלשינים על תהי תקוה וכל עושי רשעה כרגע יאבדו וכל

---

¹ That בינצרפי in b. Sabb. 116a is the same as בינצרני is only a conjecture of several scholars, which, however, cannot be defended.

² Cp. Tertullian in *Marc.* vi. 8, unde .... nos Judaei Nazaraeos appellant. Jerome, *On Sacr.*, 143, 16 (ed. Lagarde II. p. 175): et nos .... apud veteres Nazaraei dicebamur.

³ V. M. Bloch, *Institutionen des Judenthums*, I. 193.

The Jews in the Works of the Church Fathers. 133

אויבינו מהרה יכרתו, and that, instead of ולמלשינים, the word ולמינים or ולמשרתים was substituted in R Gamaliel's days, while, at a still later date, והזדים was added against the Romans.[1] I consider this supposition highly improbable. We can hardly believe that the term ולמלשינים would have been dropped, when we reflect how much cause there was in every age for the retention of a commination against the dangerous *Delatores*. Besides, the Christians cannot, in this prayer, be designated by the term מינים, which is manifestly the same as μιναῖοι or Minaei; for the Christians regarded this sect as damnable heretics, and would not have had the slightest objection to their being cursed by the Jews. The truth seems to be that the covert reference lies in the phrase וכל עושי רשעה. It is with regard to these words that the Codices of the Liturgy exhibit such numerous variations, which proves that they were not part of the original form of the prayer. Maimonides does not read וכל עושי רשעה, but וכל אפיקורסים.[2] This passage, then, is the one directed against the heretics. The modern וכל עושי רשעה, which looks so innocent, must have been adopted as a cover for the far more suspicious and dangerous expression נוצרים. So, too, in another passage (*Jerusalem Berachot*, 5d, ed. Krotoschin) the expression רשע is used as the designation of a sect תני כולל של מינים ושל הרשעים במכניע זדים. *Tosefta Berachot* iv. 25 has, instead of רשעים, the more forcible פושעים. *Massechet Derech Eretz Rabba* (beginning of chap. ii.) has הצדוקים והמסורות והרשעים; *Exodus Rabba*, c. 19, מינים ומשומדין ורשעי ישראל. In all these passages the word רשעים can only refer to a sect. I believe that the second phrase read originally וכל הנוצרים כרגע יאבדו. As, however, נוצרי was primarily the title of Jesus, the earlier Fathers were correct in asserting that the Jews cursed Jesus, inasmuch as the expression may refer equally

---

[1] *Revue des Etudes Juives*, xiv. 30.
[2] Derenbourg, *ibid*.

to Jesus or to Christianity. As in their time Christians and Nazarenes were still identical, they had no need to explain the difference of designation. In Epiphanius' and Jerome's days the Nazarenes were only a sect, and no longer formed the whole of Catholic Christendom. These Fathers found it, therefore, necessary to say that the Jews in their formula of malediction cursed the Nazarenes, but meant the Christians.

Thus the accounts of the Church Fathers on this head are harmonised.

Returning to Justin, we note that Agadic elements are to be found in his writings in considerable quantity; most of them have been thoroughly discussed by Goldfahn in his essay, "Justin Martyr and the Agada." (Graetz's *Monatsschrift* xxii., 1873, and in a separate reprint.)

II.

CLEMENT OF ALEXANDRIA.

The writings of Titus Flavius Clemens of Alexandria offer but few materials of interest for Jewish literature. His distinguishing excellence consisted in a sound knowledge of Hellenic literature rather than of theology. His information about Judaism he seems to have derived exclusively from Greek writings, particularly from Philo and Josephus. A persecution of the Christians, which raged in Alexandria in the years 202 and 203, drove Clement to seek safety in flight, and he appears to have taken up his residence for a short while in Syria (Euseb. *H. E.*, VI. 11). Here he may have gleaned something from the Jews at first hand. Of Hebrew he was not altogether ignorant. Most of his explanations of terms are indeed unfortunate, and argue little for an intimate knowledge of the language. But that he possessed a certain acquaintance with Hebrew is proved by the prolix remarks found in his writings on the

The Jews in the Works of the Church Fathers. 135

characteristics which distinguish Hebrew from other languages.[1] It should also be borne in mind that his quotations sometimes differ from the Septuagint, and this variation would seem to show that he consulted the original text.[2] Only on the supposition that Clement had a command of Hebrew can we account for the fact that he criticises adversely those who, when reading Scripture, pervert its plain meaning by their tones, and place a forced construction on clear and wise laws by their transposition of points and accents.[3] That this reproach is aimed at the Jews is obvious. And it is a valuable testimony, from a comparatively early period, to the free and unrestricted manner in which the text of Holy Writ was handled for Agadic purposes.

Hostile expressions against the Jews are not found in his writings. His essay Κανὼν ἐκκλησιαστικὸς ἢ πρὸς τοὺς Ἰουδαΐζοντας (Euseb. *H. E.*, VI., 13) may have contained some; but the work, with the exception of a few fragments, is lost. He argues that the Jews have no right to twit Christianity with its numerous sects, seeing that Judaism is also rent by factions, but that nevertheless its professors strive their hardest to win converts.[4] He betrays his contempt by the anxiety which he expresses in his exposition not to be confounded with the vulgar Jews.[5] Apart

---

[1] *Strom.* vi. 15 (viii. 353, M.), Ἔχει δ' οὖν καὶ ἄλλας τινὰς ἰδιότητας ἡ Ἑβραίων διάλεκτος, καθάπερ καὶ ἑκάστη τῶν λοιπῶν . . . .

[2] A striking deviation in the translation of Leviticus xi. 13, 14 (Deut xiv. 12) is noticeable, Ἀλλ' οὐδ' ἰκτῖνα ἢ ὠκύπτερον μαστοφαγῇ ἢ ἀετὸν φαγεῖν φησίν . . . . *Paed.* iii. 11 (viii. 653, M.). The words ὠκύπτερον μαστοφαγῇ are wanting in the LXX.

[3] *Strom.* iii. 4, end (viii. 1144), Οὗτοι εἰσὶν οἱ κατὰ τὴν ἀνάγωσιν φωνῆς τόνῳ διαστρέφοντες τὰς Γραφὰς πρὸς τὰς ἰδίας ἡδονάς, καί τινων προσῳδιῶν καὶ στιγμῶν μεταθέσει τὰ παραγγελθέντα σωφρόνως τε καὶ συμφερόντως βιαζόμενοι πρὸς ἡδυπαθείας τὰς ἑαυτῶν.

[4] *Ib.*. viii. 15 (ix. 524, M.), πρὸς τὰ ὑπὸ Ἑλλήνων καὶ Ἰουδαίων ἐπιφερόμενα ἡμῖν ἐγκλήματα ἀπολογησάσθαι . . . . Πρὸς οὓς φαμέν· Ὅτι καὶ παρ' ὑμῖν τοῖς Ἰουδαίοις . . . . πάμπολλοι γεγόνασιν αἱρέσεις· καὶ οὐ δήπου φατὲ δεῖν ὀκνεῖν . . . . ἰουδαΐζειν.

[5] *Ib.* vii. 8 (ix. 553, M.), Ἰουδαίων τῶν χυδαίων.

from these isolated instances, he is a defender of Judaism rather than an antagonist. In his Stromata an endeavour is made to prove that the Greek philosophers obtained their wisdom from Jewish teachers, and that the Jewish law stands higher than Hellenic law.

Agadic elements are more plentiful in Clement's writings than the course of his studies would naturally lead us to expect. He lays great value on the traditions of the true and hidden sense of Scripture[1] preserved by Jewish teachers, whom he knows as the μύσται, a term probably current in Alexandria.[2] As he, however, usually quotes traditions without naming the μύσται in connection with them, it is a matter of some difficulty to distinguish in his writings those elements which are of specifically Jewish origin. But as a proof that his works do contain genuine Jewish traditions I quote the following specimens. He tells us (*Strom.* I. 23, viii. 900 M.) on the authority of the μύσται, that Moses slew the Egyptian with a "mere" word, φασὶ δὲ οἱ μύσται λόγῳ μόνῳ ἀνελεῖν τὸν Αἰγύπτιον. This is identical with the well-known tradition which explains the text (Exod. ii. 14) הלהרגני אתה אומר as meaning that Moses pronounced the Ineffable Name, and thereby destroyed the Egyptian taskmaster. (See *Exodus Rabba*, and Rashi *ad locum*.)

Clement notes (*ibid.* viii., 897 M.), that the law-giver had several Hebrew names besides his Egyptian one—Moses; his parents called him at his circumcision יהויקים;[3] and after his death he received, according to the Mystae, a new name, Μελχί (מלכי ?). This is undoubtedly a genuine Jewish Agada; though I cannot, at present, trace its parallel in

---

[1] *Strom.* i. 12 (viii. 753, M.), τὰς ἀποκρύφους τῆς ἀληθοῦς γνωσίως παραδόσεις . . . .

[2] *Vide infra.*

[3] This observation is also noteworthy from a sociological point of view; we are thereby informed that already in the second century it was customary among the Jews to give their sons names on the occasion of their circumcision (but see Luke i., 59).

Jewish sources. There is a discussion in T. B. *Sota*, 12a, and *Exod. R.* 1, between some Tanaites on the name Moses[1]; but there is no hint of Jehojakim, or of the name conferred upon the leader after his death. It should also be noticed that the phrase μετὰ τὴν ἀνάληψιν implies another Agada; that Moses, like Enoch and Elijah, did not die, but was translated to heaven. This legend is clearly alluded to in Jude, verses 8, 9. It is also found in detail in *Deut. R.*, *ad finem* Babylonian Talmud *Sota* 13b, לא מת משה. Cp. also *Baba Bathra*, 17a, where it is said that Moses belonged to those against whom the angel of death was powerless, לא שלט בהם מלאך המות. Maimonides quotes the legend at the beginning of his Introduction to the Talmud.

After these undoubted specimens of Jewish Agadas we feel ourselves justified in ascribing a Jewish origin to some of Clement's obscurer legends. Clement notes, in connection with Genesis xv. 5, that Abraham, according to the opinions of some, perceived the divine wonders of the Creation and the beautiful order of nature. This exegesis is opposed to the Christian interpretation, which sees in the text a reference to Jesus, the Son of God (*Strom.* v. 1, ix. 20 M.): "Ὕστερον δὲ, ἀναβλέψας. εἰς τὸν οὐρανὸν, εἴτε τὸν υἱὸν ἐν τῷ πνεύματι ἰδών, ὡς ἐξηγοῦνταί τινες, εἴτε ἄγγελον εὔδοξον, εἴτε καὶ ἄλλως ἐπιγνοὺς Θεὸν κρείττονα τῆς ποιήσεως, καὶ πάσης τῆς αὐτῇ τάξεως.

The Midrash, commenting on the same verse (*Gen. R.*, c. 44), says that the contemplation of the star-spangled firmament made the patriarch feel himself an astrologer, which agrees with his having realised the order of nature.[2] Even the added touch that Abraham saw an angel is not merely invented by Clement; for the Midrash remarks (on verse 7) that Michael was the saviour of Abraham and would

---

[1] ר׳ מאיר אומר טוב שמו רבי יהודה אומר טוביה שמו ר׳ נחמיה אמר הגון לנביאות.

[2] נביא את ואין את אסטרולוגוס.

become ultimately the saviour of his posterity. Clement had doubtless heard this Agada, but reproduced it in the wrong place. Clement states that Buzzi, Urias the son of Samaia, and Habakkuk were Jeremiah's contemporaries. προφητεύουσι δὲ καὶ Βουζὶ καὶ Οὐρίας ὁ υἱὸς Σαμαίου καὶ Ἀμβακοὺμ σὺν αὐτῷ. Strom. i., 21 (viii., 849). Cp. Strom. i. 21 (viii., 872 M.), where Σοφωνίας Βουζὶ follow after Jeremiah. This notice is evidently based on an Agada. And, in fact, Seder Olam R., c. xx. ad finem, collates the following passages:—דבר ה' אל צפניה כו' דברי־ ירמיהו בן חלקיהו אשר היה דבר ה' אליו וכו' וגם איש היה מתנבא בשם ה' וכו' היה חיה דבר ה' אל יחזקיאל בן בוזי וכו' כולם נתנבאו סמוך לחורבן.

According to this quotation, Zephaniah, Jeremiah, Uriah (Jerem. xvi. 20), and Ezekiel were contemporary prophets; this is in complete agreement with Clement. We are thus also in a position to identify Clement's enigmatic Buzi—who has given this Father's editors so much trouble—with Ezekiel, son of Buzi. Either "Ezekiel" has dropped out, or his father is really meant, in accordance with the tradition that where a prophet's father is named, he too was a prophet.

Graetz, in his *Hagadische Elementen bei den Kirchenvätern* (Fränkel's *Monatsschrift*, III., 1854, p. 311), first drew attention to the agreement between Clement and the *Seder Olam Rabbi*. I will give one more striking instance. Clement says, *Strom*. i., 21 (viii., 842 M.), that Elisha commenced to prophesy at the age of forty, and prophesied for a period of six years. Whence is this statement, which is given with as much emphasis as if it rested on Scriptural authority, derived? The *Seder Olam R*., c. xix., says:—מכאן אתה מחשב כמה שנים פרנס אלישע את ישראל־־־־־־יותר מששים שנה. Undoubtedly we ought to read in the Greek, not ἕξ, but ἑξήκοντα (instead of ξ', equal to 60, ς', equal to 6, was written by mistake). This tradition, then, Clement has in common with the Seder Olam. That Elisha commenced his prophetic career at the age of forty we do not find in any of the Jewish sources; it must nevertheless have been a common tradition, and the same supposition would account for many other of Clement's statements. In conclusion, we may note that this Father was acquainted with many more traditions than he gives. He, for example, alludes to an exposition of the Mystae in connection with the sacrificial ritual, but does not say anything more definite about it.

III.

ORIGEN.

Origen was born, probably, in Alexandria, about 185 or 186 A.D. It is generally assumed that his parents were Christians, but this was probably the case on one side only. His father's name, Leonides, has been preserved, but not that of his mother. This omission is not accidental, but is due to the reverence of pious Christian writers for Origen's memory, which led them to suppress his mother's name on account of her Jewish descent.[1] The fact that she knew enough of Hebrew to teach her son,[2] and that he occupied himself with the study of that language, contrary —according to Jerome—to the usage of his nation and age, are strong evidence in favour of this view.[3] His impulse to Hebrew studies he probably received from his Jewish mother.[4] In his capacity as Bishop of Cæsarea, in Palestine, Origen must have come into frequent contact with learned Jews, as indeed appears from his writings. He mentions again and again his *Magister Hebraeus*, on whose authority he gives several Agadas.[5] His depen-

---

[1] *Strom.* ii. 20 (viii. 872, M.), δι' αἰτίας ἃς ἴσασιν οἱ μύσται.

[2] Jerome, *Ep.* xxxix. *ad Paulam*, c. 1, Tum vero quod in Origine quoque illo Graecia tota miratur, in paucis non- dicam mensibus, sed diebus, ita Hebraeae linguae vicerat difficultates, ut *in discendis canendisque Psalmis cum matre contenderet*.

[3] Cp. Smith-Wace, *op..cit.*, iv. 976.

[4] Jerome, *De viris illustr.* 54, contra aetatis gentisque suae naturam.

[5] *De Princ.*, 1, 3, 4, iv. 26 ; in the Greek Fragment, ὁ Ἑβραῖος. I may

dence on Jewish masters is already emphatically noted by Jerome.[1] He often mentions the views of the Jews, by which phrase he refers not to the teaching of certain individuals, but to the method of exegesis universally prevalent among the Hebrews of his time.[2] Those of them with whom he cultivated personal intercourse were distinguished by their scientific attainments. The one Jew whom he names is no less considerable a personage than Hillel, the Patriarch's son, or Jullos, as Origen calls him.[3] His other Jewish acquaintances were either closely related to the patriarch's family or occupied a high position on account of their erudition.[4] No wonder that with such opponents Origen carefully avoids, in his polemic, offensive expressions; forming, in this respect, a noble exception to the usual practice of the Church fathers. Origen fights principles, not their representatives or exponents. Occasionally, however, a harsh sentence against his Jewish antagonists escapes him.[5] He even ventures to assert that the Jews of his time could no longer boast of men of real knowledge.[6] Consistently with this adverse judgment, Origen labours chiefly to refute the scriptural exposition of Jewish teachers, and to establish in lieu thereof his own exegesis. He not only had private interviews with Jewish

---

remark here that I give my quotations in Greek when the original writings of Origen remain, and in Latin when only the Latin translation has survived.

[1] Jerome, *Lib.* i. *adv. Ruff.*, c. 13 ; cp. the Introduction supra.

[2] *E.g., Ep. ad Africanus* § 12, φασὶ δὲ οἱ Ἑβραῖοι. For other quotations see infra.

[3] My especial authority for this is Graetz's "*Hillel, the son of the Patriarchs*" (*Monatsschrift* xxx., 1881, p. 433, etc.). My revered teacher, Professor W. Bacher, in his *Hagada of the Palestinian Amoraim*, i. 92 and 107 § 2, suggests the hypothesis that Origen also had intercourse with Hoschja.

[4] Grätz, *op. cit.*

[5] *Hom.* x. *in Jerem.* § 8 (xiii. 368, M.), βλέπετε αὐτῶν τὰς καρδίας διεσθιομένας ὑπὸ τῶν δυνάμεων ἀντικειμένων.

[6] *Ib.* § 3 (xvii. 361, Gr. Text is not clear), Neque magistri neque doctores in Judaea aliqui remanserunt: et licet sint innumerabiles qui sibi sapientiam vindicent, non est jam sermo Dei in eis.

teachers, but also engaged in public disputations in the presence of large audiences, which included among their ranks competent controversialists. This we gather from several expressions in his writings.[1] The principal topics discussed at these meetings may be summarised as follows:—

1. *The Scriptural Text.*—The copies of the Bible that circulated among the Christians were, as we have already had occasion to remark, corrupt in several passages. At a disputation between Jews and Christians, the former, naturally enough, alluded to these mistakes, and mocked their opponents for allowing such obvious blunders. This kind of argument, the first beginnings of which we have traced in Justin, plays an important part in Origen. The wish to free the Church from the just reproaches of the Jews on this score, led him to undertake that gigantic enterprise, the fruit of which is the Hexapla.[2]

2. *The Apocrypha.*—Another point of difference was the

---

[1] *Contra Celsum* I. 45 (xi. 744, M.), Μέμνημ'αι δέ ποτε ἔν τινι πρὸς Ἰουδαίων λεγομένους σοφοὺς διαλέξει χρησάμενος τοιούτῳ λόγῳ, πλειόνων κρινόντων τὸ λεγόμενον. *Ib.* I. 55 (xi. 761, M.), Μέμνηναι δέ ποτε, ἔν τινι πρὸς τους λεγομένους παρὰ Ἰουδαίοις σοφοὺς ἐνζητήσει ταῖς προφητείαις ταύταις (*Jesaja* liii.) χρησάμενος· ἐφ' οἷς ἔλεγεν ὁ Ἰουδαῖος.... *Ib.* i. 56 (xi. 764, M.), καὶ μέμνημαί γε πάνυ θλίψας τὸν Ἰουδαῖον νομιζόμενον σοφὸν ἐκ τῆς λέξεως ταύτης· ὃς πρὸς αὐτὴν ἀπορῶν, εἶπε τὰ τῷ ἑαυτοῦ Ἰουδαϊσμῷ ἀκόλουθα, etc., etc.

[2] Epiphanius, *De ponderibus et mensuris*, c. 2, Ὠριγένης .... ἀποκατέστησε τῷ ἑκάστῳ τόπῳ τὸν ἐλλείποντα λογον .... ἵνα μὴ παραλείψῃ Ἰουδαῖος καὶ Σαμαρείταις ἐπιλαμβάνεσθαι τῶν ἐν ταῖς ἁγίαις Ἐκκλησίαις θείων Γραφῶν—Ruffinus lib. v. Invect. adv. Hieronymum, c. 4, Apostatae quidem et Judaei interpretati sunt ea, quorum lectione Judaei maxime utuntur. Et quia frequenter si disputatio incidisset, vel immutata esse aliquanta, vel deesse, vel abundare in nostris Scripturis mentiebantur, voluit *Origenes* nostris ostendere, qualis apud Judaeos Scripturarum lectio teneretur .... ut sciremus non quid nobis, sed quid Judaeis adversum nos certantibus aut deesse, aut abundare videntur. Origen recurs frequently to the Jewish method of reading, *e.g.*, *Hom. in Num.* xvi. 4, Hebraei habere se scriptum dicunt.— *Comm. in Ep. ad Rom.* lib. ii. § 13 (xiv. 909, M.), ipsi in Hebraeis exemplaribus habere se dicunt ....

Apocrypha, to which the Church attached an exaggerated importance, notwithstanding its frequent want of taste and silliness, over which the Jews could only make merry. The history of Susanna was always derided by them for this reason.[1] The Jews had an Apocrypha of their own, which they valued; but this seems to have been distinguished from what we term Agada only in as far as it was already written down, while most other Agadas were still orally circulated.[2] Origen draws no distinction between the Jewish Apocrypha and Jewish traditions, knowing that they merged into one.[3] It is especially noteworthy that he also knew of the existence of certain mystic writings, by which he could not have meant either Apocrypha or Agada, for both these classes of literature were known to him under their proper names.[4] He must have been thinking of such works as treat of the מעשה מרכבה, or מעשה בראשית, etc., writings which, according to

---

[1] *Epistola ad Africanum de historia Susannae* § 5, ʼΑσκοῦμεν δὲ μὴ ἀγνοεῖν καὶ τὰς [sc. γραφάς] παρ' ἐκείνοις, ἵνα, πρὸς Ἰουδαίους διαλεγόμενοι, μὴ προφέρωμεν αὐτοῖς τὰ μὴ κείμενα ἐν τοῖς ἀντιγράφοις αὐτῶν, καὶ ἵνα συγχρησώμεθα τοῖς φερομένοις παρ' ἐκείνοις· εἰ καὶ ἐν τοῖς ἡμετέροις οὐ κεῖται βιβλίοις· τοιαύτης γὰρ οὔσης ἡμῶν τῆς πρὸς αὐτοὺς ἐν ταῖς ζητήσεσι παρασκευῆς, οὐ καταφρονήσουσιν, οὐδ' ὡς ἔθος αὐτοῖς, γελάσονται τοὺς ἀπὸ τῶν ἐθνῶν πιστεύοντας ὡς ἀληθῆ, καὶ παρ' αὐτοῖς ἀναγεγραμμένα ἀγνοοῦντας.—*Ib*. § 4, Ὥρα τοίνυν εἰ μὴ λανθάνει ὑμᾶς τὰ τοιαῦτα, ἀθετεῖν τὰ ἐν ταῖς Ἐκκλησίαις φερόμενα ἀντίγραφα, καὶ νομοτεθῆσαι τῇ ἀδελφότητι, ἀποθέσθαι μὲν τὰς παρ' αὐτοῖς ἐπιφερομενας ἱερὰς βίβλους, κολακεύειν δὲ Ἰουδαίους, καὶ πείθειν, ἵνα μεταδῶσιν ἡμῖν τῶν καθαρῶν, καὶ μηδὲν πλάσμα ἐχόντων.—From these concessions may be observed how weak the Church felt itself at that time. Later on the victorious Church used quite a different language.

[2] *Ib*. § 9, Σαφὲς δ' ὅτι αἱ παραδόσεις λέγουσι πεπρίσθαι Ἡσαΐαν τὸν προφήτην. καὶ ἐν τινι ἀποκρύφῳ τοῦτο φέρεται. A Hagada, therefore, which existed in an *apocryphon*, *i.e.* which was established in writing. Probably it is a reference to Ἀναβατικὸν Ἡσαΐου, which is mentioned several times.

[3] In Matt. xvii. 2 (xii. 1477, M.), εἴτε ἐκ παραδοσέων, εἴτε καὶ ἐπιβάλλον τις, εἴτε καὶ ἐξ ἀποκρύφων ....

[4] *In Matt. Comm. ser.* § 28 (xiii. 1636, M.), Ex libris secretioribus, qui apud Judaeos feruntur ....

the Talmud, were wont to be withheld from the uninitiated and especially from Christians and heretics.

3. *Christian Dogmas.*—The mysterious birth of Christ still formed a point of controversy between Jews and Christians. Justin, who knew that the Jews could not and would not accept Christ's divinity, also touches on this theme.[1] Origen reports a far harsher judgment as the belief of the Jews. He says in his commentary on John xx. 14 (xiv., 608 M.), that the Jews spoke after the following fashion: Ἡμεῖς μᾶλλον ἕνα πατέρα ἔχομεν τὸν Θεὸν ἤπερ σύ, ὁ φάσκων μὲν ἐκ παρθένου γεγεννῆσθαι, ἐκ πορνείας γὲ γεγεννημένος. Jesus' illegitimate birth was always a firmly held dogma in Judaism, which found clear expression in its ancient and modern literature, passed over to the heathens of antiquity and lives to-day in the consciousness of every simple-minded Jew, who only knows as much on this subject as he has learnt from his parents. Must not this conviction have found expression in the Talmud? Has that monumental work, which contains such valuable evidence on the events of the first Christian centuries, nothing to tell us concerning this Jewish dogma? Certainly it has. The Talmud here agrees with Origen. The founder of the dominant creed it calls ישו בר פנדרא, or ישו פנדרא.[2] What does פנדרא mean? Although much has been written about this term, its significance and etymology have not been fixed. I here suggest an explanation, quite different from those hitherto proposed. In Sifri Deut., § 320, תהפוכות (Deut. xxxii. 20) is thus interpreted, הפכפכנים הם פורנים הם, "They are a common and degraded people." פורנים is the Hebrew transcription, with the plural suffix, of the Greek πόρνοι, as Levy (*Neuhebr. Wörterb.*, iv. 18a) correctly states. The Greek term πόρνος has become naturalised in the Rabbinic

---

[1] *Dial.* c. 49 (vi. 581, M.), ὁ Τρύφων . . . . καὶ γὰρ πάντες ἡμεῖς τὸν Χριστὸν ἄνθρωπον ἐξ ἀνθρώπων προσδοκῶμεν γενήσεσθαι.

[2] Also פנטרא, which is even written פנתרא.

dialect, in which πορνεῖον and πόρνη also occur. Now, this passage in the Sifri has, as a *varia lectio*, פרדנים. Levy gives πόρδων as its equivalent, but this has nothing in common with πόρνοι. We believe that a purely phonetic phenomenon accounts for this variant. Between the liquids "r" and "n," the dental "d" has been inserted, a procedure familiar to philologists. פרדנים is thus the same as πόρνοι. The feminine form πόρνη shows a similar phonetic transformation in the word פרדנית.[1] We now arrive at the conclusion of this chain of reasoning. פנדרא and פרדנית (disregarding the feminine suffix) only differ in the relative position of the liquids "n" and "r." That these frequently change their places in the Rabbinic dialect in the case of words borrowed from the Greek is well known. It may therefore be confidently assumed that פנדרא is nothing but πόρνη, modified by phonetic influences. ישו בר פנדרא would thus mean Jesus, the son of the prostitute, or in Origen's phrase ὁ ἐκ πορνείας γεγεννημένος, or as the Pesikta Rabbathi has it ברא דזניתא. This explanation sums up the beliefs held in Jewish circles concerning Jesus.[2] This does not shut out the view that the present form of the word פנדרא, which sounds like παρθένος, may also have been influenced by the Christian dogma that Jesus was the son of a virgin. The opposition between ἐκ παρθένου and ἐκ πορνείας forms even in Origen a sort of play upon words, and Jewish popular wit was probably not slow to take advantage of the similarity of sound.

4. *Abrogation of the Mosaic Law.*—The Pauline doctrine that Jesus' advent superseded the Law of Moses encountered a lively opposition down to the third century. The contradiction between Christ's declaration that not an iota of the Law shall be given up, and his followers' disregard of the

---

[1] This disagrees with the view of Levy, iv. 102a.

[2] I think it unnecessary to cite the Rabbinical passages relating to Jesus, as they are accessible in the Essay of Laible, *Jesus Christus im Talmud* (Berlin, 1891).

most essential Jewish observances was too glaring not to be noticed and severely reprehended by impartial heathens, who told the Christians that their spiritual conception of the Scriptures did not justify their neglect of the ceremonial laws; for there were Jews who also conceived their law spiritually and yet scrupulously practised all of them.[1] Origen nevertheless pours out the vials of his contempt on Jews "after the flesh."[2] He finds it unnecessary to wash the hands before meals; the sole requisite is spiritual purity.[3] The fulfilment of the laws in a spiritual sense sometimes assumes a very comical aspect!

Origen brings against the Jews a charge already met with in Justin; viz., that the Jews falsify and mutilate the Scriptures.[4] He is convinced that there is a want of agreement between the old and new copies of the Jewish Bible, and that much which exhibited a Christian tendency in the former, has been disfigured in the latter.[5] He is unconscious that he is here guilty of a self-contradiction; for he often admits that the Jews possess the genuine, the Christians the corrupt text of Holy Writ.[6] Especially instructive is Origen's testimony to the great attraction which Judaism possessed for the heathens. There must have been still many proselytes to Judaism in his day;

---

[1] *Contra Celsum* I. § 1 (xi. 793, M.), μηδὲ τοῦτο κατανοήσας, ὅτι οἱ ἀπὸ Ἰουδαίων εἰς τὸν Ἰησοῦν πιστεύοντες οὐ καταλελοίπασι τὸν πάτριον νόμον. Origen adds to this (§ 3), The Jew of Celsus ought rather to have said, τινὲς δὲ (ὑμῶν) καὶ διηγούμενοι ὡς ἐπαγγέλλεσθε, πνευματικῶς, οὐδὲν ἧττον τὰ πάτρια τηρεῖτε.

[2] *Comm. in Matt.* xi. 12 (xiii. 939, M.), οἱ σωματικοὶ Ἰουδαῖοι.

[3] *Ib.* xi. 8 (xiii. 928, M.), Ὤιοντο γὰρ κοινὰς μὲν καὶ ἀκαθάρτους εἶναι, χεῖρας τὰς τῶν μὴ νιψαμένων πρὸ τοῦ ἀρτοφαγεῖν . . . . Ἡμεῖς δὲ οὐ κατὰ τὴν τῶν παρ' ἐκείνοις πρεσβυτέρων παράδοσιν . . . . καθαίρειν πειρώμεθα . . . .

[4] *Hom. in Jerem.* xvi. 10 (viii. 451, M.), Judaei qui exemplaria nonnulla falsarunt.—The Greek text is here damaged.

[5] *In Matt. Comm. ser.* § 28 (xiii. 1636, M.) in Scripturis *veteribus* quae legebantur in Synagogis eorum.

[6] *Hom. in Jerem.* xvi. 10 (xiii. 450, M.), Εἶτα ἄλλη ἐστὶ προφητεία, ἣν οὐκ οἶδ' ὅπως παρὰ τοῖς Ἑβδομήκοντα οὐχ' εὕρομεν δὲ ἐν ταῖς ἐκδόσεσι, δηλονότι κειμένην ἐν τῷ Ἑβραικῷ . . . .

otherwise there is no adequate reason for the vehement indignation with which he attacks the Judaizers, forgetting himself so far as to utter curses and imprecations, altogether unworthy of him, against those who were converted to the old faith.[1] Among the Christians, too, there were several "Judaizers." Many, especially women, kept the Sabbath on the same day of the week as the Jews; washed and adorned themselves in honour of the day.[2] Origen maintains that the Sabbath in the "carnal" sense, as the Jews conceive it, cannot possibly be observed; to carry out its ordinances literally, one would have to abide in the same place for twenty-four hours, without stirring. This point was often treated in controversies. It forms, even in Jerome's writings, the subject of a lively dispute between Jews and Christians.[3] Besides the Sabbath, the Passover

---

[1] *In Matt. Comm. ser.* § 16 (xiii. 1621, M.), Arbitror ergo omnem hominem qui ex conversatione gentili Judaeorum factus est proselytus, filium gehennae fuisse et priusquam proselytus efficiatur.

[2] *Hom. in Jerem.* xii. 13 (xvii. 396, M.), Καὶ περὶ σαββάτου γυναῖκες μὴ ἀκούσωσι τοῦ προφητοῦ, οὐκ ἀκούουσι κεκρυμμένως, ἀλλὰ ἀκούουσι φανερῶς. Οὐ λούονται τὴν ἡμέραν τοῦ σαββάτου....

[3] *Comm. in Ep. ad Rom.* vi. 2 (xiv. 1094, M), Quid enim tam impossibile, quam Sabbati observatio secundum litteram Legis, ut in multis saepe jam diximus? Jubetur enim non exire de domo sua, non se movere de loco suo, nihil oneris levare. Quae quia impossibilia vident Judaei, qui secundum carnem legem observant, inepta quaedam et ridicula commentantur, quibus impossibilitatem Legis sarcire videantur. Origen omits to tell us what these stupidities are. We discover them, however, through Jerome, *Ep. ad Algasiam*, c. 10 (iv. 207, ed. Martianay), Praeterea quia jussum est, ut diebus Sabbathorum sedeat unusquisque in domo sua, et non egrediatur, neque ambulet de loco, in quo *habitat, si quando eos juxta litteras experimur arctare*, ut non jaceant, non ambulent, non stent, sed tantum sedeant, sic velint praecepta servare, solent respondere et dicere: *Barachibas et Simon et Helles magistri nostri tradiderunt nobis, ut bis mille pedes ambulemus in Sabbatho*, et cetera istiusmodi. The answer of the Jew would probably in the original Hebrew run as follows: קבלה היא בידנו מפי ר׳ עקיבה משום ר׳ שמעון שאמר הלל, etc. In the Talmud and Midrash we frequently note apologetic utterance against the reproach of the Christians in reference to the keeping of the Sabbath, of which a few have been collected by N. Brüll, *Grätz Jubelschrift*, p. 191, N. 1. The laws concerning circumcision were declared by

was also kept according to Jewish rites by numerous Christians who prepared unleavened bread.[1] Origen asserts, that this sympathy with Judaism was not spontaneous, but was the artificial work of missionaries, who carried on a zealous propaganda on behalf of the ancient faith, and cajoled Christians to practise its rites.[2]

Origen has a large number of Hebrew traditions or Agadas; in this respect he stands, among the Church Fathers, second only to Jerome. It should be noted that Origen knows Jewish traditions which have reference to the Gospels. He gives, in the name of the Jews, an explanation of the term κορβᾶν, קרבן, which occurs in the New Testament.[3] Iscariot, Judas the traitor's surname, also seems to have had a traditional, though erroneous, Jewish interpretation.[4] His account of the Tetragrammaton and of the word pronounced in its stead, points to a genuine Jewish tradition.[5] The Midrashim or Agadas, in the strict sense of the terms, which Origen quotes so profusely, he probably owed to his intercourse with distinguished Jewish friends.

Origen as impossible as those concerning the keeping of the Sabbath. See on that point Diestel, *History of the Old Testament*, p. 27, and Bacher, *Ag. of the Pal. Amor.*, I. 92, N. 4.

[1] *Hom. in Jerem.* xii. 13 (xiii. 396, M.), "Ὅσοι ἐν ὑμῖν (ἐγγὺς γάρ ἐστι τὸ πάσχα) ἄζυμα ἄγετε. I quote the text with some emendations.

[2] *In Matt. Comm. ser.* § 16 (xiii. 1621, M.), [Judaei] diligenter circumeunt plurima loca mundi, ut advenas Judaizare suadeant.

[3] *Comm. in Matt.* xi. 9 (xiii. 929, M.), οἱ δὲ φαρισαῖοι καὶ οἱ γραμματεῖς τοιαύτην ἐναντιουμένην τῷ νόμῳ παράδοσιν ἐκδεδώκασιν, ἀσαφέστερον ἐν τῷ Εὐαγγελίῳ κειμένην, ᾗ οὐδ' αὐτοὶ ἐπιβεβλήκαμεν ἄν, εἰ μὴ τῶν 'Εβραίων τις ἐπιδέδωκεν ἡμῖν τὰ κατὰ τὸν τόπον οὕτως ἔχοντα .... Κορβᾶν ἐστι ὃ ὀφείλεις μοι, τουτέστι, δῶρον. The same words, but not in the name of the Jew, are also found in *Theophylactus in Matt.* xv. 5.

[4] *In Matt. Comm. ser.* §78 (xiii. 1727, M.), Audivi quendam exponentem patriam proditoris Judae secundum interpretationem Hebraicam *exsuffocatum* vocari.

[5] *Selecta in Psalm* ii. (xii. 1104, M.), κύριον γὰρ ἐνθάδε ἀντὶ τοῦ Ἰαὴ εἴρηκεν, καὶ ἔστιν ἡ ἀρχὴ τοῦ ψαλμοῦ παρ' Ἐβραίοις " Ἀλληλουΐα". ἔστι δέ τι τετραγράμματον ἀνεκφώνητον παρ' αὐτοῖς, ὅπερ καὶ ἐπὶ τοῦ πετάλου τοῦ χρυσοῦ τοῦ ἀρχιερέως ἀναγέγραπται, καὶ λέγεται μὲν τῇ Ἀδωναΐ προσηγορίᾳ, οὐχὶ τούτου γεγραμμένου ἐν τῷ τετραγραμμάτῳ.

His introductions to some of these Agadas show that he had a certain respect for them.[1] Most of them are also to be found in Jewish sources. Some have already been compared by Graetz in his *Hagadische Elemente bei den Kirchenvätern*. We will confine our attention to a few selected specimens, which will serve to show how useful it would be to collect and investigate the Agadas scattered through Origen's writings.

1.—"The Garden of Eden, the Centre of the World."

Selecta in Gen. ii. 8 (xii. 100, M.), Οὐκοῦν παραδεδώκασιν Ἑβραῖοι, ὅτι ὁ τόπος ἐν ᾧ ἐφύτευσεν τὸν παράδεισον ἢ τὸν κῆπον Κύριος ὁ Θεός, Ἐδὲμ καλεῖται· καὶ φάσιν αὐτὸν μέσον εἶναι τοῦ κόσμου, ὡς κόρην ὀφθαλμοῦ· διὸ καὶ τὸν ποταμὸν τὸν Φείσων, ἑρμηνεύεσθαι στόμα κόρης, ὡς ἐκ τοῦ Ἐδὲμ ἐκπορευομένου τοῦ ποταμοῦ τοῦ πρώτου.

A remarkable Midrash of which I have failed to find an exact counterpart in Jewish writings. It may be a conclusion drawn from the old assumption that Palestine is the centre of the earth, while Eden was supposed to be in or near to Palestine. The precise situation of Paradise forms the subject of a Talmudic controversy. T. B. *Erubin*, 19a:—
גן עדן א'ר ר'ש לקיש אם בארץ ישראל הוא בית שאן פיתחה ואם בערביא בית גרם פיתחא. On the other hand, Midrash Ps. xxi. 3, tells us: שערי גן עדן סמוכין להר המוריה. The interpretation of פישון as פי אישון is unknown to me in Jewish sources.

2.—Potiphar and Joseph.

Origen says in a *catena regia*, quoted from a MS. in Montfaucon's Hexapla on Genesis xxxvii. 36: "Phutirpharem eundem ipsum esse tradunt, qui Josephi herus et socer

---

[1] *Hom. in Isajam* I. § 5 (xiii. 225, M.), Cur non dicamus in praesenti traditionem quandam Judaeorum verisimilem quidem, nec tamen veram .... It is a reference to the well-known tradition of the murder of the prophet Isaiah.

fuit. Narrantque Aseneth illam matrem suam apud patrem accusasse, quod insidias in Josephum struxisset, non autem ab eo insidiis appetita fuisset. Quam ille Josepho sponsam dedit"...... The same tradition is given more explicitly in Jerome, *Quest. Heb.*, in Gen. xxxvii. 36: "Putiphar eunucho. Ubi quæritur, quomodo postea uxorem habere dicatur. Tradunt Hebræi emptum ab hoc Joseph ob nimiam pulchritudinem in turpe ministerium, et a Domino virilibus ejus arefactis, postea electum esse juxta morem Hierophantarum in pontificatum Neilopoleos, et hujus filiam esse Aseneth, quam postea Joseph uxorem acceperit."[1]

Three features are to be distinguished in these notices, (*a*) Potiphar, Gen. xxxvii. 36, is identified with Potipherah, Gen. xli. 45, and Asenath is, accordingly, Joseph's former master's daughter; (*b*) Asenath, according to this account, felt and evinced sympathy with her father's slave before his imprisonment; (*c*) Potiphar, inflamed by the sight of Joseph's beauty, contemplated the commission of an unnatural crime, but was stricken with impotence. The whole of this tradition, with the exception of the second part, which does not really belong to it, occurs in Jewish sources. We read in T. B. *Sota*, 136:—ויקנהו פוטיפר אמר רב שקנאו לעצמו [בא גבריאל וכרכו] בא גבריאל ופירעו מעיקרא כתיב פוטיפר ולבסוף פוטיפרע. The words placed within brackets are erased by Rashi, because they are tautologous. R. Nathan, of the *Aruch*, retains them, and explains, סירכו לבצים ופירעו לגיד. This view is obviously preferable to Rashi's. The words סריס פרעה form the basis of the interpretation סירכו ופירעו. We thus have here the express tradition that Potiphar is identical with Potipherah, and was stricken with impotence as a punishment for his evil intentions towards Joseph.

The same legend is recorded in other portions of Rabbinic literature. *Gen. R.*, c. 86, פוטיפר שהיה פורע עצמו לע"ז

---

[1] This tradition is not found in Rahmer's *Hebrew Traditions in the Works of Hieronymus*, Breslau, 1861.

כיון שייחד חפר לשם נעשה פוטנן סריס פרעה שנסתרס מלמד
שלא לקחו אלא להשמיש וסירסו הקב״ח בגופו. Levy, *Neuhebr.
Wörterbuch*, and Fürst, *Glossarium Græco-hebræum*, p. 163 *b.*,
give φωτεινός as the Greek original of פוטנן. Kohut's *Aruch
Completum*, VI., 315*b*, agrees with Perles' *Rabbinische Sprach-
u. Sagen-Kunde*, p. 21, that פוטנן is derived from πουτάνα=
putana. Both explanations are incorrect; for φωτεινός would
imply a eulogy of Potiphar, where none was intended by the
Midrash, and "putana" is not Latin but Romaic. I venture
to suggest that פוטנן=σπάδων, a eunuch; σπάδων is the
rendering of סריס, which the Septuagint and Vulgate give
generally as well as Gen. xxxvii. 36, in the particular passage
under discussion (see H. Rönsch, *Itala u. Vulgata*, second
edition, p. 246). The name פוטיפרע, which sounded so
strange to the Hebrew ear demanded an Agadic interpretation. It was accordingly bisected; the first half, פוטי,
was explained in three ways: (*a*) as derived from פטם,
Gen. R., c. 86, שחיה מפטם עגלים לע״ז; (*b*) from φῶς
"light," *Tanchuma* II., וישב, § 16, למה נקרא שמו פוטיפר
שהבהיק לביתו של פרעה,[1] cp. *Jelamdenu*, quoted in *Aruch*,
s. v., פט II., פוטיאל שהאיר במעשים טובים שאת אומר ביוונית
פוטיא; (*c*) from σπάδων, a "eunuch," *Gen. R.*, ib., where the
words סריס פרעה are added to confirm the derivation. פרע,
the second component of the name, was interpreted in two
ways: (*a*) as derived from פרע, to untie or loosen, *Gen. R.*,
ib., שחיה פורע עצמו לע״ז; (*b*) from פרע, to cut out, T. B.
Sota, 13*b*, בא גבריאל ופירעו. Musafia, in *Kohut* I. 211, was
guided by a right instinct when he adds וי״מ שהוא מסרס.
He also thought of σπάδων. Our interpretation is confirmed
by a passage in *Shir R.* I. 1, בל יתיצב לפני חשוכים זה
פוטיפר שהחשיך הקב״ח עיניו וסירסו. This completely ex-
cludes the idea of Potiphar's enlightenment, or, according
to Fürst, *ibid.*, his conversion. In the *Tanchuma*, Potiphar

---

[1] The passage שנכנס לביתו של פרעה ונעשה ביתו פוטינום should be
emended into כיון שנכנס יוסף לביתו נעשה [פוטיפרע] פוטנן, according
to *Gen. Rab.* and *Yalkut*.

is not represented as the enlightened but as the enlightener, *i. e.*, the steward over Pharaoh's house, an office which has no obvious connection with *spiritual* enlightenment.

3.—DIVISION OF THE RED SEA INTO TWELVE PARTS.

Hom. in Exod. v. 5 (xii. 330, M.), Audivi a majoribus traditum, quod in ista digressione maris, singulis quibusque tribubus filiorum Israel, singulæ aquarum divisiones factæ sunt, et propria unicuique tribui in mari aperta est via, idque ostendi ex eo, quod in Psalmis (cxxxv. 13) scriptum est: *Qui divisit mare rubrum in divisiones.* Per quod multæ divisiones docentur factæ, non una. Sed et per hoc quod dicitur: Ita Benjamin junior in stupore...... (Psalm. lxviii. 28) nihilominus unicuique tribui propius enumerari videtur ingressus. Hæc a majoribus observata in Scripturis divinis, religiosum credidi non tacere. Cp. Eusebius Comm. in Ps. lxxvii. 13 (xxiii. 113, M.), φασὶ γοῦν Ἑβραίων παῖδες εἰς ιβ' τμήματα διῃρῆσθαι αὐτὴν κατ' ἀριθμὸν τῶν ιβ' φυλῶν τοῦ λαοῦ.

Every detail of this Midrash is found with wonderful similarity in the Jewish sources.

The division of the Red Sea into twelve parts, corresponding to the number of the tribes, is recounted in the *Mechilta* (Exod. xiv. 16) נחלק לשנים עשר גזרים. In Midrash on Psalm cxxxvi. 15, in Yalkut Habakkuk, § 565, and in Yalkut Exodus, § 245, נחלק לשנים is a mistake for י"ב ל' עשר. Even the verse with which this tradition is connected is the same in Origen and the Midrash. In the *Mechilta* (Exod. xiv. 15), the passage commencing מהו אומר לגוזר ים סוף לגזרים, breaks off abruptly. The expected conclusion is the deduction that the sea was divided into twelve parts. Maimonides knew this Midrash in its full form. Commentary on *Aboth* V. 4: שנבקעו לדרכים רבים כמספר השבטים והוא אמרו לגוזר וכו'. In *Aboth de R. Nathan*, c. XXXIII. (v. I.), the circumstance is added that the tribes expressly stipulated that the sea should be divided into sections, אמר להם משה קומו עברו

אמרו לא נעבור עד שנעשה לפנינו גזרים שנאמר לגזור וכו'.
Ps. lxviii. 28, from which, Origen says, the same tradition is derived, is connected with it in the *Mechilta*, ibid. 6, *Sota*, 36b, Midrash on Ps. lxviii. 14, where we read that the tribes disputed as to which of them was to be the first to pass through the Red Sea; the result could only have been that they crossed simultaneously by different routes.

4.—REPENTANCE OF KORAH'S SONS.

Comm. in Ep. ad Rom. x. 7 (xiv. 1262, M.), Non puto absurdum videri si ea quæ nobis de his etiam in veteri Testamento a patribus rationabiliter tradita sunt, his scilicet, qui ex Hebræis ad Christi fidem venerunt, in medium proferamus. Aiebant ergo tres illos filios Core, quorum nomina invenimus in Exodo (vi. 24)...... Aser...... Elchana...... et Abiasaph......, cum pater eorum Core pecasset una cum Dathan et Abiram...... istos segregasse a cœtu nefario et ab impia conspiratione sequestratos unanimiter ad Deum precem pœnitentiæ profudisse: atque exauditos a Deo non solum veniam pœnæ, sed et prophetiæ gratiam meruisse, et hoc quoque eis a deo poscentibus esse præstitum, ne quid triste aut exitiabile prophetare juberentur: et ob hoc omnes psalmos quicunque nominibus eorum attitulati referuntur, nihil triste adversum peccatores aut asperum continere.

Only that part of this beautiful Agada which refers to the repentance of Korah's sons is to be found in Jewish sources. A passage in Midrash to Ps. xlv. 4, runs as follows:—כך בני
קרח לא היו יכולין לומר שירה לפני הק'ב'ה בפיהם עד שרחש
לכם וקבלם מיד ולמה לא היו יכולין לומר שירה בפיהם לפי
שהיתה שאול פתוחה מתחתיהם ואש בלהטת סביבותיהם:
The שירה here mentioned is parallel to Origen's *preces pœnitentiæ*. This elucidates the passage in T. B. *Sanhedrin*, 110a (*Megilla*, 14a):—מקום נהבצר להם בגיחנם וישבו עליו ואמרו
שירה. That this Agada is ancient appears from the unfamiliar word נהבצר; cp. also Midrash on Psalms i. 5, and xlv. 1. In the Jewish sources we miss the fine touches of the gift of prophecy bestowed on Korah's sons, and of

the always comforting nature of the Korachide Psalms. Perhaps others will be fortunate enough to discover these points too.

5.—Israel's Strength consists in Prayer.

Hom. in Num., xiii. 5 (xii. 672, M.), Ut autem scias tale aliquid cogitasser egem (Balak), ex scripturae verbis intellige, quæ ego a magistro quodam, qui ex Hebræis crediderat, exposita didici. Scriptum est ergo (Num. xxii. 4): *Et dixit Moab ad seniores Madjan : Nunc, ablinget synagoga hæc omnes, qui in circuitu nostro sunt, sicut ablingit vitulus herbam campi.* Aiebat ergo magister ille, qui ex Hebræis crediderat: Cur, inquit, tali usus est exemplo, dicens: sicut ablingit vitulus herbam campi? Ob hoc sine dubio, quia vitulus ore obrumpit herbam de campo et lingua tanquam falce quæcunque invenerit, secat. Ita ergo et populus hic, quasi vitulus ore et labiis pugnat, et arma habet in verbis ac precibus. Haec igitur sciens rex mittit ad Balaam, ut et ipse deferat verbis verba contraria et precibus preces.

This is a well-known Midrash. *Sifri* Num. xxii. 4, § 157; *Num. R.* c. 20, 3; *Tanchuma* II.; בלק, § 4; Rashi, *ad locum*: מה שור כחו בפיו אף הם כחם בפיהם.

6.—Phineas and Elijah identical.

Comm. in Joann. vi. 7 (xiv. 225, M.), Οἱ Ἑβραῖοι παραδιδόασι Φινεές τὸν Ἐλεαζάρου υἱὸν . . . . αὐτὸν εἶναι Ἠλίαν καὶ ἀθάνατον ἐν τοῖς Ἀριθμοῖς αὐτῷ διὰ τῆς ὀνομαζομένης εἰρήνης ἐπηγγέλθαι.

Jerome knows the same tradition, which he thinks the Jews took from an apocryphal work. Eliam esse Phineas Hebræi ex Apocryphis persuasum habent (V. 813 Vallarsi). The sentence, פנחס הוא אליהו is only found in *Yalkut Num.* 772, in the name of R. Simeon b. Lakish and ascribed to a Midrash as its original source. Its preservation in a miscellaneous collection is noteworthy. The ordinary Midrashim seem to have purposely suppressed it, because it smacked of Apocrypha. Its omission is particularly noticeable in

Tanchuma II., פנחס, § 3: לכן אמור לו חנני נותן לו את
בריתי שלום וכן הוא אומר בריתי היתה אתו הזחיים והשלום,
which, as it stands, makes no sense. The *Yalkut*, ib., on
the basis of Malachi ii. 5, infers that the peace promised Phineas was eternal life: ונתן לו חיי העולם הזה וחיי
העולם הבא ונתן לו שכר טוב והיתה לו ולזרעו אחריו ברית
כהונת עולם. Here, too, Origen, gives the correct tradition
that Phineas' immortality is implied in the word שלום.

7.—ALLEGORICAL INTERPRETATION OF THE SERAPHIM.

De Princ. I. 3, 4 (xi. 143, M.), Ἔλεγε δὲ ὁ Ἑβραῖος τὰ ἐν
τῷ Ἡσαΐᾳ δύο σεραφὶμ ἑξαπτέρυγα κεκραγότα ἕτερον πρὸς
ἕτερον . . . . τὸν Μονογενῆ εἶναι τοῦ θεοῦ καὶ τὸ Πνεῦμα τὸ
ἅγιον. Cp. *De Princ.* iv. 26 (xi. 400, M.), Nam et Hebræus
doctor ista tradebat: pro eo quod initium omnium vel finis
non possit ab ullo comprehendi, nisi tantummodo a Domino
Jesu Christo, et a Spirito sancto, aiebat per figuram visio-
nis Isaiam dixisse, duos seraphim solos esse, qui duabus
quidem alis operiunt faciem Dei, duabus vero pedes, et duabus
volant clamantes ad invicem sibi dicentes: Sanctus, sanctus, sanctus, etc. The same tradition was also known to
Jerome, in Ep. xli. (lxv.) *Ad Pammachium et Oceanum*,
who, however, rightly stigmatizes it as an odious and
godless exposition. Had it not been expressly so stated,
one could hardly believe that a Jew said it. The Christian
terms, at least, are to be placed to a Church Father's
account. I could not find this interpretation in the
Jewish sources, and none will regret its absence.

8.—DANIEL, CHANANIAH, MISHAEL AND AZARIAH
WERE EUNUCHS.

Comm. in Matt. xv. 5 (xiii. 1225, M.), Φασὶ δὲ Ἑβραίων
παῖδες τὸν Δανιὴλ καὶ τοὺς τρεῖς σὺν αὐτῷ Ἀνανίαν, Ἀζαρίαν
Μισαήλ, ἐν Βαβυλῶνι εὐνουχίσθαι, πληρουμένης τῆς πρὸς
τὸν Ἐζεκίαν εἰρημένης προφητείας ὑπὸ Ἡσαΐου ἐν τῷ "Ἀπὸ
τοῦ σπέρματός σου λήψονται, καὶ ποιήσουσι σπαδόντας ἐν τῷ
οἴκῳ τοῦ βασιλέως Βαβυλῶνος" (Is. xxxix. 7). Φασὶ δὲ ὅτι

περὶ τούτων καὶ Ἡσαίας ἐπροφήτευσε φάσκων " Μὴ λεγέτω ὁ ἀλλογενής ὁ προσκείμενος κυρίῳ. ἀφοριεῖ μὲ ἄρα κύριος ἀπὸ τοῦ λαοῦ αὐτοῦ," καὶ τὰ ἑξῆς, ἕως τοῦ " κρείττονα υἱῶν καὶ θυγατέρων " (Is. lvi. 35).

Origen gives the tradition with more fulness of detail in *Hom.* in Ezek. iv., § 8 (xiii. 703, M.). On Ezek. xiv. 15: Audivi quondam a quodam Hebræo hunc locum exponente atque dicente, ideo hos nominatos, quia unusquisque eorum (Daniel, Job, Noe) tria tempora viderit, lætum, triste et rursum lætum...... Noe...... vidit mundum ante diluvium ......in diluvio......, rursum in resurrectione omnium peccatorum. Dicit mihi aliquis: concedo de Noe, ut tria tempora viderit: quid respondebis mihi de Daniele? Et hic ante captivitatem in patria floruit nobilitate, et deinceps in Babylonem translatus *eunuchus effectus est*, ut manifeste ex libro illius intelligi potest; vidit et reversionem in Jerusalem. Ut autem probetur quod ante captivitatem eunuchus factus sit, assumamus id quod ad Ezechiam dictum est (Is. xxix. 7)...... Job...... fuit locuples...... deinde accepit diabolus potestatem adversus eum;...... post hæc apparet ei Dominus. *Ib.* § 5 (xiii. 700, M.). Daniel qui traditus est eunuchorum principi cum Anania, Azaria, Misaela, eunuchus fuit...... Quomodo filii Danielis docebuntur, quem eunuchum fuisse Judæi tradunt? Verum quia fertilis et sancta fuit anima illius, et propheticis divinisque sermonibus multos liberos procreavit...... Catena Regia in Prophetas ad Ezek. xiv. 5: **Υἱοὺς ἔχει ὁ Δανιὴλ κατὰ τὴν αὐτὴν πνευματικὴν γένναν, οὓς ἐγέννησεν ἡ προφητεία αὐτοῦ. υἱοὺς γὰρ σαρκικοὺς οὐκ ἔσχεν. Εὐνοῦχος γὰρ ἦν, ὥς φασι.**

The same tradition we find in Jerome lib. I., adv. Jovin., c. 25: Superfluum est de Daniele dicere, cum Hebræi usque hodie autument et illum et tres pueros fuisse eunuchos, ex illa dei sententia (II. Reg. xx. 18)......

Jerome on Daniel i. 3: Unde et arbitrantur Hebræi Danielem et Azariam et Ananiam et Misaelem fuisse eunuchos......Epiphanius, *de Vitis Prophetarum* (xliv. 424, M. ser gr.): **Καὶ ἦν' ἀνὴρ σώφρων, ὥστε θαυμάζειν τοὺς Ἰου-**

δαίους πιστεύοντας εἰς αὐτὸν εἶναι σπαδόντα. Later Church Fathers also give the same tradition, which they have however drawn from Origen and Jerome.

This Agada is widely disseminated in Jewish literature. All the details correspond; the statement that Daniel and his companions were eunuchs; the verse from which this is deduced; the question how they could have afterwards begotten children, etc. We read in B. *Sanhedrin*, 93*b* :—
ומבניך אשר יצאו ממך אשר תוליד יקחו והיו סריסים בהיכל מלך בבל רב אמר סריסים ממש...... מאי טוב מבנים ומבנות ......מבנים שהיו להם כבר ומרו From which we see that this tradition did not survive in the popular consciousness; it is stated as simply an individual opinion. Of the many views enunciated, the most noteworthy is R. Jochanan's, *ib*. 93*a* : עלו [חנניה משאל ועזריה] לארץ ישראל ונשאו נשים והולידו בנים ובנות. This, as Rashi remarks, stands in direct opposition to the above. Cp. *Gen. R*., c. 99; *Num. R*., c. 13; *Esther R*., c. 4; *Pirke de R. E*., c. LII.

9.—Moses, Author of Eleven Psalms.

Selecta in Psalmos, p. 514 (xii. 1055, M.), "Ὕστερον δὲ κινούμενος περὶ τινων λογίων Θεοῦ Ἰουλλῷ τῷ πατριάρχῃ καί τινι τῶν χρηματιζόντων παρὰ Ἰουδαίοις σοφῶν ἀκήκοα, ὅτι δι' ὅλης τῆς βίβλου ψαλμῶν .... οἱ παρ' Ἑβραίοις ἀνεπίγραφοι ἢ ἐπιγραφὴν μὲν ἔχοντες, οὐχὶ δὲ τὸ ὄνομα τοῦ γράψαντος, ἐκείνου εἰσὶν οὗ τὸ ὄνομα φέρεται ἐν τῷ πρὸ τούτων ἐπιγραφὴν ἔχοντι ψαλμῷ. καὶ περὶ τούτων λέγων, πρότερον μὲν ἔφασκεν, ὅτι τρισκαίδεκα εἰσὶν ὁ του Μωυσέως εἶτα δὲ ἐξ ὧν ἀκήκοα καὶ αὐτὸς .... τὴν ἀνέφερον ἐπ' αὐτὸν, ὅτι εἰσὶν ἕνδεκα, εἶτα πυθόμενος, τοῦ παρ' αὐτοῖς δοκοῦντος σοφοῦ, ἐμάνθανον, ὅτι εἶεν ἕνδεκα.

Jerome, *adv. Ruff*., c. 13, quotes the whole of this passage. He knows the tradition of Moses' authorship, gives it, however, not in the name of the Jews, but as a firmly established and self-evident truth:—Qui [Moses] non solum nobis quinque reliquit libros,...... sed undecim quoque Psalmos, ab octogesimo nono [LXX.]...... usque ad nonagesimum nonum. Quod autem in plerisque codicibus nonagesimus octavus habet titulum *Psalmus David*, in Hebraico non habetur, hanc habente scriptura sancta consuetudinem, ut omnes psalmi qui cujus sint titulos non habent, his deputentur, quorum in prioribus psalmis nomina continentur (Ep. cxl. ad Cyprianum, c. 2).

This Midrash also is found in Jewish sources; *Pesikta de R. Kahana*, 198a, ed. Buber: אחד עשר מזמורים אמר משה כנגד אחד עשר שבטים שבירך ואלו חן......אמר ר' יהושוע עד כאן שמעתי מכאן ואילך את מחשב לעצמך. R. Joshua's words imply that this was an ancient tradition. It is found also in Midrash on Psalm xc. 3, *Yalkut Ps.*, § 841, Rashi to Psalm xc. 1; cp. Midrash on Psalm xc. 4: אחד עשר מזמורים שאמר משה בטכסים של נביאים אמרן.

10.—BEASTS AS EXECUTORS OF DIVINE PUNISHMENT.

Hom. in Ezek. iv. 7 (xiii. 701, M.), and *in Ezek.* xiv. 4: Aiunt etiam Judæi, si quando lupi homines devoraverint impetum facientes in domos, et cæteræ bestiæ, ut historia refert leones quondam in humanum genus immissos, et alio tempore ursos (II. Reg. xvii. 2) istius modi devorationes ex Dei indignatione descendere.

I have not found a parallel in Jewish sources, but the root idea is patent and needs no special tradition.

S. KRAUSS.

(*To be Continued.*)

THE JEWS IN THE WORKS OF THE CHURCH FATHERS.

IV.

EUSEBIUS.

EUSEBIUS, whose best work was accomplished on Palestinian soil, in Cæsarea, must often have come into contact with Jews, and been instructed by them on several points.

He is bitterer in tone against the Jews than Origen. "Jew," with him, is a term of opprobrium. He repeatedly calls his opponent Marcellus a Jew (*Eccles. Theol.* II. 2, 3). The phrase, "one of the circumcised,"[1] which he employs, likewise covers a world of scorn and contempt. His work, *Demonstratio Evangelica*, was avowedly written as a direct attack on the Jews.[2] He holds that, in their exposition of Scripture, the Jews are guilty of serious errors, and efforts should be made to induce them to abandon their heresies; that is to say: Religious disputations should be encouraged with the view of persuading them to give up their faith.[3]

Eusebius regards the condition of the Jews as lamentable. What they felt most bitterly was the harsh law which denied them the solace of visiting the holy city of Jerusalem. He describes the wailing and weeping of the poor Jews when they caught even a distant glimpse of Zion's ruins.[4]

---

[1] *Dem. Ev.* i. 6 (xxii. 49, M.), τις τῶν ἐκ περιτομῆς.

[2] *Ib.* i. 1, 11, οὐ ... κατὰ 'Ιουδαίων, ἄπαγε, πολλοῦ γε καὶ δεῖ ...

[3] *Ib.* iv. 16 (xxii. 317, M.), Διόπερ εἰκὸς τοὺς ἐκ περιτομῆς ἀποσφάλλεσθαι ...

[4] *Comm. in Psalm* lviii. 7-12 (xxiii. 541, M.), Διὸ εἰσέτι καὶ σήμερον ἀμφὶ μὲν τοὺς ὅρους καὶ κύκλω παριόντες πόρρωθεν ἵστανται μηδ' ἐξ ἀπόπτου

The Jews in the Works of the Church Fathers. 83

Eusebius was as much under the influence of Jewish tradition as his predecessors and several of his successors. It has nearly the same authority with him as the Scriptures, and he calls it ἄγραφος παράδοσις = " unwritten tradition."[1] Its depositaries he terms δευτερρταί,[2] and he characterises them in the following happy fashion : "There are people gifted with an uncommon strength of intellect ; and whose faculties have been trained to penetrate to the very heart of Scripture. The children of the Hebrews call them δευτερωταί, because they expound Holy Writ."[3] Eusebius also distinguishes between esoteric and exoteric exegesis. The Agadas he frequently classes with the exoteric exposition.[4] Though there is no clear statement to that effect, we may confidently assume that Eusebius enjoyed direct intercourse with Jews. Cæsarea, the Father's residence, was inhabited by learned Hebrews; and we know from the Talmud that disputations between Jews and Christians were frequent in this town. It will also clearly appear from passages to be hereafter quoted, that Eusebius had a Jewish teacher. His Agadas, of which we give a few specimens, he owed to Jews.

τὸ πάλαι νενομισμένον αὐτοῖς ἱερὸν ἔδαφος θεάσασθαι καταξιούμενοι, ἔξωθεν δὲ κυκλοῦντες, πίστιν ἐπάγουσι τὴν ... Γραφῇ (Ps. liii. 7).— *Ib.* lxix. 26—29 (xxiii. 153, M.), Ἰουδαίων δὲ οὐδένα τολμῶντα ἐπιβαίνειν τῇ πόλει, μήτε γε οἰκεῖν αὐτόθι. ἀλλ' οὐδὲ οἴκησις Ἰουδαϊκὴ περιλέλειπται ἐν τῷ τόπῳ, ὡς τινα τῶν Ἑλλήνων οἰκεῖν ἐν αὐτῇ δύνασθαι.

[1] *Hist. Ev.* iv. 22 (xx. 384, M.), ἐκ Ἰουδαϊκῆς ἀγράφου παραδόσεως.

[2] *Praep. Ev.* xi. 5 (xxi. 852, M.), Δευτερωταί ... οὕτω δὲ φίλον τοὺς ἐξηγητὰς τῶν παρ' αὐτοῖς Γραφῶν ὀνομάζειν.

[3] *Ib.* xii. 1 (xxi. 952, M.), τοῖς ... τὴν ἕξιν προβεβηκόσι, καὶ πολιοῖς τὰ φρόνημα, ἐμβαθύνειν καὶ δοκιμάζειν τὸν νοῦν τῶν λεγομένων ἐπιτέτραπται. Τουτοὺς δὲ παισὶν Ἑβραίων Δευτερωτὰς φίλον ἦν ὀνομάζειν ὥσπερ ἑρμηνευτὰς καὶ ἐξηγητὰς ὄντας τῆς τῶν Γραφῶν διανοίας.

[4] *Dem. Ev.* vi. 18 (xxii. 461, M.), ὁ δέ γε Ἰώσηπος καὶ τὰς ἔξωθεν Ἰουδαϊκὰς δευτερώσεις ἀπηκριβωκώς ... ἐπάκουσον. The subject here discussed is the earthquake, the legend concerning which is to be found in the *Seder Olam.*, c. xx. ובעמוס הוא אומר שנתים לפני הרעש ובישעיה הוא אומר ב'שנת מות המלך עזיהו כו' והוא היה ביום הרעש שנאמר וינועו אמות הספים.

1.—ABRAHAM OBEYED THE PRECEPTS OF THE TORAH BEFORE THE REVELATION.

Demonstratio Evang. I. 6. Μεμαρτύρηται γοῦν τὰ προστάγματα καὶ τὰς ἐντολὰς, τά τε δικαιώματα καὶ τὰ νόμιμα τοῦ θεοῦ, πρὸ τῆς Μωσέως διαταγῆς πεφυλαγμένος. Eusebius infers this from Gen. xxvi. 3, 4, 5.

This is one of the best known Agadas, cp. T. B. Joma, 28b:—אמר רב קיים אברהם כל התורה כלה שנאמר עקב אשר שמע. Even the verse on which the statement is based is the same in the Father and the Talmud. Compare *Baba Meziah,* 85b and 87a, where R. Meir already asserts: אברהם אבינו אוכל חולין בטהרה היה.

2.—KING HEZEKIAH'S SIN.

Commentary on Isaiah xxxix. 1. (VI. 362 M.). συνεξετάξουσιν ἡμῖν καὶ διερευνωμένοις τὰ κατὰ τοὺς παρόντας τόπους, ὁ τῶν Ἰουδαίων διδάσκαλος ἔλεγεν νενοσηκέναι μὲν τον Ἐζεκίαν, ἐπεὶ μὴ εἰρήκει ᾠδὴν εἰς τὸν θεὸν εὐχαριστήριον ἐπὶ τῇ πτώσει τῶν Ἀσσυρίων, ὡς Μωϋσῆς ᾖδεν ἐπὶ τῇ ἀπωλείᾳ τῶν Αἰγυπτίων καὶ ὡς Δεβόρρα ἐπὶ τῃ ἀπωλεία τοῦ Σισάρα καὶ ὡς Ἄννα ἐπὶ τῇ γεννήσει του Σαμουήλ.

Jerome, *ad locum*, quotes the same tradition.

This Agada, which is already noteworthy for the direct statement prefacing it—that Eusebius learnt it from his Jewish teacher—is one of the most widely disseminated in Jewish literature. The reflection that Hezekiah was guilty of ingratitude in not chanting a hymn of praise to God after Sennacherib's fall, also occurs in T. B. *Sanhedrin,* 94a: למרבה המשרה ולשלום אין קץ ׳ אמר ר׳ תנחום דרש בר קפרא בציפורי מפני מה כל מ״ם שבאמצע תיבה פתוח וזה סרום בקש הקב״ה לעשות חזקיה משיח וסנחריב גוג ומגוג ׳ אמר מדת הדין לפני הקב״ה ומה דוד מלך ישראל שאמר כמה שירות ותושבחות לפניך לא עשירתו משיח חזקיה שעשית לו כל הנסים

Ib., הללו ולא אמר שירה לפניך תעשה משיח ׳ לכך נסתתם
גנאי הוא לחזקיה וסיעתו שלא אמרו שירה.

In *Exodus R.*, c. 18, and T. B. *Pesachim*, 117a, it is related that Hezekiah sang a hymn of praise (Hallel) before the destruction of the Assyrian hordes, but there is no hint of his having been censured for omitting to sing one after the occurrence. In *Shir R.*, on c. IV. v. 8, an excuse is put into Hezekiah's mouth:—ראוי היה חזקיה לומר שירה על מפלת סנחריב אמר חזקיה תורה שאני עוסק בה מכפרת על השירה.

In *Echa R.*, c. I., the excuse takes the following form:— חזקיה אמר אין בי כח······לומר שירה. From all these passages it is obvious that Hezekiah's omission to compose a special hymn of praise largely exercised the imagination of the Agadists. In T. J. *Pesachim*, towards the end, a dictum is found, couched in so authoritative a form that it sounds almost like an Halacha, to the effect that a miraculous deliverance should be followed by a thanksgiving:—כשהקב״ה עושה לכם נסים תהיו אומרין שירה. To this the cogent objection is raised that Mordecai and Esther did not sing a hymn after Haman's fall. *Jalkut*, on Isaiah, § 306, quotes a passage from the lost Jelamdenu, in which the duty of a thanksgiving is deduced from Exodus xv. 1: ויאמרו לאמר לדורות. A contrast is also drawn between the songs of Moses, Deborah and David, and Hezekiah's culpable negligence—a feature also dwelt upon in Eusebius. In all the above passages, however, we miss the detail, found in the Father's recital of the legend, that Hezekiah's sickness was a Divine punishment for his omission of a thanksgiving. Nevertheless, this, too, comes from a Jewish source. The following passage is excerpted from Jelamdenu by the Jalkut on 2 Kings, § 243:—
כשעלה סנחריב עליו והפילו האלהים לפניו הוה ליה למימר שירה על מפלתו ולא אמר ומה היה לו והפילו האלהים במטה כדי שיאמר שירה שנאמר מכתב לחזקיהו.

This legend illustrates the advantages that would accrue from a systematic history of the Agada. Such a history is however only possible after a comparison of all available auxiliary sources, among which the Church Fathers occupy an important place.

3.—BERODACH BALADAN AND HEZEKIAH.

Comm. in Is. xxix. 1 (vi. 361 M.) τὸν δὲ Βαβυλώνιον ἐγνωκέναι τὴν ἀπὸ τῆς νόσου ῥῶσιν αὐτοῦ καὶ ἀπεσταλκέναι πρὸς αὐτὸν ἄνδρας......ἐπειδὴ συνέβη τὴν ἡμέραν ἐκείνην καθ' ἣν τὸ σημεῖον τῆς τοῦ ἡλίου ἀναδρομῆς ὡρῶν γεγενῆσθαι διπλασίων, μὴ γάρ λατεῖν τοῦ το τοὺς Βαβυλωνίους δεινοὺς ὄντας περὶ τὴν τῶν ἄστρων δε ὡρίαν καὶ......συνεῖδον ὡς ὑπὸ κρείττονος περιηνέχθη εἰς τουπισὼ δυναμέως ...... ταῦτα μὲν ὁ Ἑβραῖος.

The same Agada is given in Ephraem Syrus' work (*Op. Syr.* I. 562, 563 R.) on 2 Kings xx. 10, as one of Jacob Edessenus' *Scholia*. It is introduced in the following impressive phrases :—במלא חלין סוכלא מטשיא אית דלו לכל נש ידיע ודאן זדקא דלגליא אנא איתוחי דא אמר אנא. Graetz has discussed the latter passage in the *Monatsschrift*, 1854, p. 383. The Agada inspires him, however, with but little respect, because it is not given by Ephraem but by Jacob Edessenus, who belongs to a later period. The passage in the commentary on the parallel chapter in Isaiah, which is, indeed, given in Ephraem's name, Graetz suspects to have been interpolated from Jacob Edessenus' *Scholion*. The historian has however overlooked the fact that the earlier Father, Eusebius, also has this Agada. By the time it reached Edessenus, it had received several additions, *e.g.*, the recital of the miracle of the turning back of the sun by the Ninevite Jews to the Babylonian king; and the statement that his native Jewish subjects enlightened him as to Hezekiah's importance. The Agada, in the form in which Eusebius presents it, is found in Jewish sources. Thus T. B. *Sanhedrin*, 96a:—בעת ההיא שלח בראדך בלאדן······משום כי חלה חזקיה ויחזיק שדר ליה ? ורשב חשמש עשר מעלות······א'ל מאי

The Jews in the Works of the Church Fathers. 87

האי א'ל חזקה חלש ואיתפח אמר איכא גברא כי האי ולא בעינא
לשדורי ליה שלמא. The detail is, however, wanting that
the Babylonians, by their knowledge of astronomy, discovered that the sun-dial had turned back. We read,
instead, in a passage excerpted from the Pesikta (*Jalkut*,
2 Kings, § 244) another account of the manner in which
the Babylonians were apprised of the miracle. מרודך בן
יבלאדן היה למוד לאכול בשש שעות וישן עד תשע שעות
וכיון שחזר גלגל חמה ישן לו ועמד ומצאו שחרית בקש להרוג
את כל עבדיו אמר הנחתם אותי לישן כל היום וכל הלילה
אמרו ליה מרי יומא הוא דהדר ביה ואלוהו של חזקיה החזירו
אמר להם איכה כי האי גברא כו'.

We must confess that the Church Father's narrative, *viz.*, that the Babylonians discovered the miracle by their astronomical calculations, is more reasonable than the Jalkut legend. Here is another illustration of the usefulness of foreign sources for the purpose of rectifying the Agadas, so many of which sound strange.

4.—THE TRAITOR SHEBNA.

Comm. in Is. xii. 10, 11 (VI. 249 M.). Ἔλεγε τοίνυν ὁ Ἑβραῖος ἀρχιερέα γεγενῆσθαι τὸν Σομνάν (שבנא) τρυφητὴν τινα καὶ τὸν βίον ἄσεμνον ἄνδρα, ὡς καὶ προδοῦναι τὸν λαόν.

Jerome comments on the passage "Supra diximus Sobnam fuisse pontificem qui Assyriis prodidat civitatem, sed quia hoc traditionis est Hebraicæ et Scriptura non loquitur..."

All the details of this Agada recur in Jewish sources. Thus, *Leviticus R.*, c. 5, זה שבנא כהן גדול היה. Shebna's treachery is discussed in T. B. *Sanhedrin* 26a. Eusebius's brief suggestion that Shebna was sensual (τρυφητής) is repeated in T. B. *Sanhedrin*, 26a, אמר ר' אלעזר שבנא בעל הנאה היה כתיב הכא בא אל הסוכן וכתיב התם ותהי לו סוכנת.

This somewhat obscure passage Rashi explains in the following gloss, כמשמעו וי״א משכב זכר. After what the Father tells us, we must decide that the explanation of the יש אומרים hits the correct sense of the Agada.

5.—Interpretation of Zech. xi. 8.

The text ואכחיד את שלשת הרעים בירח אחד received, from a very early period, the following Christological interpretation: That, after Jesus' advent, the three powerful estates, Sovereignty, Priesthood and Prophecy, disappeared from Israel's midst. This explanation recurs in Eusebius, *Dem. Ev.* X. 1 (XX. 747 M.). Jerome (on Zech. xi. 8) quotes it only to reject it. His sound common sense leads him to prefer the Jewish exegesis, which applies the text to Moses, Aaron and Miriam. Strange to say, he does not give it in the Jews' name, as Graetz already noted in the *Monatssch.* 1854, p. 189. The historian has neglected to consult the older authority, Eusebius, whom Jerome follows in so many places. It is clearly evident from Eusebius, *ibid.*, that this exegesis was not specially Jewish, but was general at that period. The passage quoted by Graetz from T. B. *Taanith* 9a:—ואכחיד את שלשת הרעים בירח אחד וכי בירח אחד מתו, והלא מרים מתה בניסן ואהרן באב ומשה באדר, completely coincides with *Seder Olam R.*, c. X., which first mentions the distinctive blessings these three pastors brought the people:—אהרן = עמוד ענן · משה = מן · מרים = באר.

V.

Ephraem Syrus.

In passionate hatred of the Jews, in contempt and active hostility towards the people of the covenant, Ephraem of Syria surpasses all the Church Fathers who came before

The Jews in the Works of the Church Fathers. 89

and all those who went after him. His voluminous writings are filled with rage and animosity against the Jews. He would like to destroy them with the fire of his words and to draw down upon their heads, by his prayers, the avenging lightning of an offended Deity. Whence this hatred? Whence this malignant spirit of persecution? It is difficult to find an adequate reason, especially as Ephraem hardly ever came into contact with the Jews, and therefore could never have been insulted by them. His resentment seems to have been aroused and stimulated by the marvellous power of resistance shown by the old creed. In his immediate neighbourhood, Babylon, the ancient people flourished with unexpected vigour. The serious blow which Julian the Apostate dealt Christianity, and which was indirectly of benefit to the Jews, may also have contributed to the contemporary Father's prejudice. He sought to relieve his feelings by pouring out vials of wrath on the defenceless Hebrews.

Ephraem terms the Jews טעיא גזירא, the circumcised vagabonds.[1] Judaism is a worthless vineyard that cannot bear fruit.[2] He frequently refers to their wretched condition, which he regards as a punishment sent from God.[3] Because they reviled Jesus, the Lord has banished them from their land, and and now they are condemned to wander over the whole surface of the earth.[4]

The golden hopes which the Emperor Julian's policy raised in the Jews' hearts, proved vain and illusory. As soon as Christianity triumphed, it turned with redoubled fury on its indestructible foe. After Julian's death Ephraem composed four hymns: against the Emperor Julian, the

---

[1] *Op. Syr.* II. 469. Cp. Lengerke, *De Ephraemi Syri arte Hermeneutica* (Königsberg, 1838), p. 15.

[2] See Zingerle, *Bibliothek der Kirchenväter*, II., 292.

[3] In Gen. xlix. 8 (*Op. Syr.* I., 108).

[4] In 2 *Reg.* ii. at the end (*Op. Syr.* I., 523) נרשו אנון לבד מן אתרא דלהון וזרקו להון בכל פניתא דמתעמרניתא.

Apostate; against the heresies; and against the Jews.[1] We quote from these envenomed productions the following passages: "The Jewish people broke out into maddening noise; the circumcised blew their trumpets and rejoiced that he [Julian] was a magician and worshipper of idols. They saw again the image of the beast on his [Julian's] gold pieces; they again viewed the bull of shame, and danced round it with trumpets and timbrels, for they recognised in this beast[2] their ancient golden calf. The heathen bull, imprinted on their hearts, he stamped on his coins for the delectation of the Jews, who were enamoured of him.[3] The circumcised blew their trumpets and behaved like madmen.[4] Jerusalem put to shame the accursed crucifiers who had dared to announce that they would rebuild the ruins their sins had wrought.[5] Fire broke out and destroyed the scholars who had read in Daniel that the desolation would endure for ever. Look! you (Christians) live at peace, free from the 'possessed,' free from contact with the servants of the devil."[6]

What especially exasperates Ephraem is that the Jews will not give up their hopes; notwithstanding the calamities with which they have been visited, they still cherish the firm conviction that the Future belongs to them and their religion—not to Christianity. The narrative of the two concubines who appeared before Solomon for judgment, is applied by Ephraem to the rival creeds, the Church and the Synagogue. Of the latter, he says: The Synagogue continually protests that her son is the living child and pleasing to God. She, furthermore, loudly asserts that the

---

[1] על יולינוס מלכא דאחנף ועל יֻלפנא טעיא ועל יהודיא in *S. Ephraemi Syri Carmina Nisibena*, Ed. Bickel (Lipsiae, 1866), and Overbeck, *S. Ephraemi Syri . . . . aliorumque Opera Selecta* (= O), Oxonii, 1865. The hymns are translated into German by Hahn in the periodical *Zeitschrift für Katholische Theologie*, II. 335 (Innsbruck, 1878).

[2] An allusion on a coin of Julian with an altar and a beast, being the sign of the restitution of Paganism.

[3] O. p. 8.   [4] O. p. 12.   [5] O. p. 18.   [6] O. p. 19.

The Jews in the Works of the Church Fathers. 91

Law of Moses is endowed with eternal life. Thus the Synagogue of the misguided perpetually contends with the Church of Jesus.[1] The hopes of the Jews find still more emphatic expression in the view that, as soon as the expected Messiah shall have arrived,[2] God's people will reign supreme.

It is interesting to learn the precise nature of these hopes which dominated the Jewish mind in the fourth century. A passage bearing on this subject may here be appropriately quoted from the Sermon against the Jews:—"Now, look! this people dreams that it will return; the people which angered God in all that it did awaits and demands a time when it will have satisfaction. As soon as this people hears of a return, they lift up their voices and shout, 'Jerusalem will be rebuilt!' Again and again they listen, for they long for the return. 'The fame of the capital will be great; its name will be glorious,' they repeatedly exclaim."

Very honourable to the Jews is the testimony which an embittered foe, like Ephraem, is forced to bear to the expansive power of Judaism, even at that time of severe oppression. We learn from Ephraem, as we have learnt from Justin and Origen, that the old faith received at this period numerous accessions from heathendom. Ephraem, of course, declares that the heathens are deluded by Jewish missionaries.[3]

Christianity still felt itself called upon to defend its

---

[1] In 1 *Reg.* iii. 16 (*Op. Syr.* I. 452) · תרתין נשׁין לעדתא ולכנושתא ר׳מזן
כנושתא דין .... השא מן קעיא ואמרא דברא דילה חי הו לאלהא ולה
שפר · ותוב:דנמוסא דמשא דמית חיא דלעלם יהב ליה · הי הכיל כנושתא
דטציא עם עדתא דמשיחא אמינאית נציא.

[2] In 1 *Reg.* i. 5 (*Op. Syr.* I. 441):—אלא אף ביומתן מתחזה שועליה ואית
ליה סברא דלשׁולתניה דתאבל נסק במאתיתה דהר משיחא דמסבא לה.

[3] In 2 *Reg.* xix. 1 (*Op. Syr.* I., 558): טופסא אנׁין דמכבנותהון דר׳שיעא
הנון דמנסין להימנות דחלי אלהא ומשׁדלין מחתחתין להון למשׁבק לעדתה
דמשׁיחׁא ולכנושתא דסטנא נסטון.

position against the Jews. In the Sermon against the Jews, Ephraem exhorts them: "Come let us examine the prophets and see whether their predictions have been fulfilled." From the course of the address we learn the chief points of controversy between Jews and Christians at this period. Opening with the challenge, "Let the accursed Jews search the Scriptures and become wise," Ephraem seeks, in the first place, to deduce from Gen. xlix. 10, 11, that the Jews' hopes are futile. "If Judah wields the sceptre and has an interpreter, the prophecies are not fulfilled. But if the sceptre has departed and the voice of prophecy is silent, then should the Jews be ashamed of their obstinacy and stiffneckedness." Another point of controversy was the interpretation of Zechariah ix. 9, and of Psalm viii. 3. It is easy to understand that Ephraem indirectly attacks the Jewish exegesis on several other points. The passages have been collated by Gerson, *Die Commentarien des Ephraem Syrus im Verhältniss zur Jüdischen Exegese* (Breslau, 1868), page 8. To this brochure the reader is referred.

Intrinsically Ephraem's commentaries are incomparably more valuable than those of the Church Fathers whom we have already discussed. Ephraem proceeded to the exposition of the Scriptures with a sufficient equipment of preliminary studies. In the first place he possessed a good knowledge of Hebrew. This, however, is not the general opinion. Abraham Geiger, for example, said (*Jüdische Zeitschrift*, VII. 69), "It is quite natural that Ephraem, though ignorant of Hebrew, should have interlarded his commentaries with Midrashic elements which he learnt from his intercourse with the Jews," a statement absolutely unwarranted.

Schaf, more recently (Smith-Wace's *Dictionary of Christian Biography*, II. 142), also seeks to prove from a few instances that Ephraem was unacquainted with Hebrew. Although, in itself, it does not greatly concern Jewish literature whether any individual Father of the Church knew Hebrew or not, still this point ought to be settled in order to enable

The Jews in the Works of the Church Fathers. 93

us to appraise Ephraem's efforts at their just value. It is by no means the same thing whether Jewish exegesis is criticised by a competent Hebraist or by an ignoramus. If it should turn out that Ephraem understood the Hebrew text, it is clearly unfair to charge him with rashly intruding into a domain in which he was incompetent to judge.

In his Commentaries Ephraem frequently refers to the original text. This should show whether he knew Hebrew or not. The mere reference counts for something. Neither Clement of Alexandria, nor Basil, nor Gregory of Nazianzus ever quotes the original text.

1. *Commentary on Genesis* i. 1 (*Op. Syr.* I. 116), Ephraem discusses the Hebrew word את:—

הדא ברת קלא קדימות סימא עבריתא איתיה דאיתיה סוריאית
ל. חנו דין לשמיא ולארתא לו דין ית אלא את

This remark is unobjectionable.

2. *Gen.* i. 2. He endeavours to explain the obscure תהו ובהו, according to Severus' *Excerpts*, as follows:—

תהו ובהו · הנו דן צדיא ושהיא בצחחא דין אחרנא אמר
ארעה איתיה הות לא מתחזניתא ולא מתקנתא ולא מתחזניתא
אמר איתיה הות מטל תחומא דמיא הו דקבא הוא וחשיר ליה
מן שית פנותא בדמות עולא הו דכריך בשלית אבגו מרבעא
דאמיה ולא מתקנתא מטל דלא גליןֹ הוי אפיה.

Schaf sees, in this quotation, a clear proof that Ephraem did not know what תהו ובהו meant. But when we examine the passage in question carefully, we see that the expression צדיא ושהיא, "empty and desolate" is a correct rendering. The next excerpt in Severus, to the effect that the earth was invisible because of the multitude of waters that covered it, and that this invisibility constituted an imperfection, is the expansion of a just idea, but is not intended to be taken as literal exegesis. Ephraem himself, in fact, only says, I. 6:— דאיתיה הות תהו ובהו הנו דין
דשהיא הות וצדיא.

3. *Gen.* i. 21 (I. 18). Ephraem speaks of the Behemoth— Job xl. 15 (10) and Psalm l. (xlix.) 10—as none but a sound

Hebraist could. To me it is inconceivable how Schaf can quote this passage in support of his theory. It runs as follows:—

תנינא דין רו‎ֹבא דאתבריו ואפן ללויתן נב‎ֹיא בימא מתמרין
ליה אלא לבהמות איוב ביבשא משרא לא אף דוד דעבד‎ֹא אמר
דעל אלף טורי‎ֹן איתיה מרעיתיה חנודין מרבועיתיה כבר דין
בתר דאתבריו אתפלגו לחון אתרו‎ֹתא דלויתן נאמר בימא
ובהמות ביבשא.

This rendering of Behemoth is not strange and peculiar, as Schaf supposes. The ancient translators differ as to the meaning. The Septuaginta has, in Psalms and Job, τὰ θηρία (Vulgate *jumenta*). Aquila and Theodotion, in both passages, κτήνη (Field, *Hexapla* II. 76, 173), while the *Peschito* gives in Psalms בעירא ותורא, but in Job only בהמות.

4. Schaf is guilty of a serious error in remarking that Ephraem could have had but a slight acquaintance with Hebrew, seeing that he is forced to have recourse to Syrian roots, in order to explain Hebrew words. His instance is where on Gen. xi. 29 (I. 59) the Father says:—חי דמטל שופרה אתקרית אסכה, "Sara was called Isca because of her beauty." Schaf seems to be unaware that this is an Agadic interpretation which, however, rests on the fact that in the Hebrew word a Syriac root was discerned. *Seder Olam R.* c. II., towards the end, ולמה נקרא שמה יסכה שהכל סכין ביפיה; more definitely in *Megilla*, 14a, and *Sanhedrin*, 69b, יסכה שהכל סכין ביפיה; according to another interpretation, שסכתה ברוח הקדש. (Cp. Gerson, *ib.*, p. 19, who, however, does not cite the passage from the *Seder Olam*.) In languages as closely correlated as Hebrew and Syriac, this mode of exposition is perfectly legitimate. In the *Mechilta* on Ex. xii. 4, תכסו is explained from the Syriac (לשון סורסי). Will any one assert that the author of that interpretation did not understand Hebrew? Why then should this exegesis appear strange when employed by Ephraem, especially as it is obviously homiletic and Agadic, rather than

grammatical? Compare the Syriac derivation of the names of Job's three daughters (Job xlii. 4).

5. *Gen.* xxxvi. 24 (I. 184):—חלף דאשכח מֹיא עבריא אמר׃ אשכח גנבֹרא במדברא. Ephraem's explanation here coincides with that given by Onkelos and the Samaritan version, as is already noted by J. Perles, *Meletemata Peschittoniana,* page 9.

6. In the sermon against the Jews (*Op. Syr.* III. 218), Ephraem translates the words בני אתונו (Gen. xlix. 11) " and his ass, my son." But in his commentary (I. 108, 190) the correct rendering, "the ass's colt" is twice given; and in the Sermon, too, the same rendering occurs (III. 224). This error, therefore, proves nothing against Ephraem's knowledge of Hebrew, as Schaf himself is inclined to admit.

7. *Deut.* ix. 9 (I. 273). Ephraem says:—איכא גיר דאמר דצלית דצמית כתיב בעבריא. He had, therefore, read the original text and understood it.

8. *Joshua* xv. 28 (I. 305):—ובזיוותֹ׳ח ׳ הנו קוריֹיה כד לֹא ידעו הנון דפשקו לסורתא מנא איתוהי הי ברת קלא עבריתא בזיותיה סמו. Ephraem exposes a mistake in the *Peschito* and appeals to the Hebrew text.

9. At the beginning of his commentary to the Book of Judges (I. 308), he draws a distinction between the terms שפטים and שבטים which is irreproachable.

10. *Jud.* v. 30 (I. 316) עבריא אמר ׳ חכימֹתא דדרוכתֹא עני אכותה. It is indeed surprising that he should have understood שרותיה in the sense of concubines. This may, however, be an exegetical licence and not a real mistake.

11. On 1 *Sam.* xxi. 8 (I. 376), ברת קלא עבריתא ינעצר גוניתא הי לן עם עבריא ומרניאת מתפשקא על מא דסערין אילין דעצרין לזיתא ולעֹנבא. "The word נעצר is common to Syriac and Hebrew. It specially refers to the pressing of grapes and olives." With the imperfect sources at our command we cannot tell that נעצר had not this meaning

in Hebrew. But our author has certainly a right to draw an inference from Syriac to Hebrew.

12. 2 *Kings* iii. 1 (I. 523), he explains the Hebrew term נקד.—נקדא דהרכא אמר כתבא שמאחו דמן עבריא נבה ותורגמיה ריש ל̈עותא דע̈נא חנו דמתרסא סונא דענא. No objection can be offered either to the note that here Hebrew and Syriac coincide or to the explanation suggested.

13. 2 *Kings* viii. 18 (1. 539), עבריא דין תוב סוכלא אחרנא וחפכא מחוא ׳ חנו ׳ אמר לא מאחא האחא. This is a studied reference to the Hebrew text.

We deem it unnecessary to give further proofs in support of our assertion, that Ephraem had a considerable knowledge of the sacred tongue.

We now turn to the question: What is Ephraem's relation to the Jewish Agada? After Lengerke, Gaertz and Gerson's thorough investigations, such a question might possibly be deemed superfluous; but such is not the case. That the Father incorporated with his commentaries a mass of Agadas and Midrashim is clear. But how did he come by them? Were his informants contemporary Jews, or Christians of the school of Edessa or Nisibis? All the other Church Fathers, to whom we have referred in this Essay, usually quote Agadas in the name of the Jews. Ephraem never does so. We frequently meet with such phrases as:—אית ׳ אנשא מן מפשקו̈נא ׳ אנשין מן ספ̈רא דאמרין ׳ אנשין אמרו ׳ אנשין איך משלמנותהון ׳ אנשין אמרו מן משלמנותא דקד̈מיע ׳ ברויא (Lengerke, pp. 14-20), the majority of which refer to the Jews. That he never distinctly names them shows his marked hostility. Hence it is extremely unlikely that any direct communication took place between the Jews and Ephraem. He would scarcely have so far overcome his prejudices as to associate with Jews. Of course, it is conceivable that there may have been two periods in Ephraem's life; one, when he was on intimate terms with Jews, and obtained an extensive acquaintance with their views; another, when he

The Jews in the Works of the Church Fathers. 97

avoided saying anything in their name. This is however, after all, a mere hypothesis, unsupported by historical facts. The question itself we have not sufficient information to settle.

The Agadas found in Ephraem's writings are too numerous to be exhaustively treated within the limits of the present essay. I refer the reader to the works of Lengerke, Graetz and Gerson, and will only quote a few specimens which those investigators have left unnoticed.

I. Comm. in *Exod.* xiv. 24 (*Op. Syr.* I. 215): מפשטא הי פשיטא הות ליה אידיה למשה איך הי דחות מן בהרכן בקרביה דעמלק. Moses, at the passage of the Red Sea, stretched forth his hands in the same manner as he afterwards did in the battle with Amalek. This remark is quite in the Agadic vein, though I have failed to find its parallel in the Jewish authorities.

II. 1 *Kings* iii. 5 (I. 451): אפלא בזנא אחרנא גבדא עבדיא נסבו להון בנשא רחב ורות ומעכא ברת מלכא דגשור Ephraem defends the view that heathen women could only become the wives of Jews after embracing their husbands' creed. Rahab, Ruth, and Maacha, the daughter of the king of Geshur, are given as instances. The Book of Ruth is the authority for the statement in Ruth's case; the Agada in the case of Rahab. Thus T. B. *Megilla*, 14*a*: חולדה הנביאה מבני בניה של רחב הזונה היתה...דאביירה ונסבה יהושע.

T. B. *Sebachim*, 115*b*, ואחר חמשים שנה ארגיירה.
Shir R. on I. 2, רחב שמעה וארגירה.
Ib. on VI. 2, *Exod. R.*, c. 26, הלא שמעה רחב ובאה ודבקה בך.

About Maacha's conversion I could find nothing in the Agada.

III. 2 *Sam.* xi. 14 (I. 408): אנשין מן אמרין דיואב אשתרודע מלתא דדויד עם ברת שבע... וידע הוא עלת קריתה דאוריא... איתי הכיל לעבדא מדם דאהפקד אלא לאגרתא סמה לותיה וכבר דדמה ושמה דדויד בזורה הו. "Many assert that Joab discovered David's relations with Bathsheba, and knew why Urijah had been summoned. He therefore executed the orders he had received from the king, but preserved the letter of authorisation, so as to have David's life and reputation at his mercy." Ephraem spins out the legend at great length. Joab, he tells us, wished to enact, with David, the rôle of Abner with Ishbosheth. He was also continually under the apprehension that David would call him to account for Abner's murder. The letter concerning Urijah would, he thought, save him from death and give him the upper hand. Here is undoubtedly a genuine Jewish tradition, but I have, unfortunately, been unable to trace it to Jewish sources.

IV. 2 *Kings* iv. (I. 256):— אמרין דאנתתא הדא אנהתא דעובדיא הות הו דבביתא דאחאב בנכסיא תלמידיה דאליא דפצי אנון למאא נבײן... ובכפנא תרסי אנון... דמיא מן דבא בחו שרכא יוף כספא מן בית מלכא ודאשתבק בתר מותה חובה לאנתתה "They say that this woman was the widow of Obadiah, Ahab's former steward and Elijah's disciple, who had rescued four hundred prophets from Jezebel's hands and maintained them during the famine. During the distress he had borrowed money of the royal household, and at his death the debt was still unpaid." The parallel of this beautiful Agada is found complete in every detail, in the Jewish sources. That the woman was Obadiah's wife is stated in the *Targum Jonathan* on the passage בעלי מית עבדך עובדיה. The steward's indebtedness is referred to in *Exod. R.*, c. 31:—
כספו לא נתן בנשך זה עובדיה שהיח עשיר אפוטרפוס של אחאב והוצא כל ממונו לצדקה וזן את העניים וחיה לוה בנשך מיחורם וכו׳.

We notice here an even verbal agreement between the Jewish narrative and that of Ephraem.

V. 2 *Kings* v. 1 (I. 531):— ומן מלתא הדא נסבו אנשׁין תחויתא ואמר (ואמרו?) דחנא איתוחי הו גברא הו דקטליה ביד נארא דנפק מן אידה תמימאית... אלא חלין מן תחויתא שרירתא גליזין אנון. "Hence many derived the fable that this [Naaman] was the man who had accidentally slain [Ahab] with an arrow." This noteworthy Agada I could find nowhere else.

VI. 2 *Kings* iv. 35 (I. 529, 530):—אסברו אנשין מן ספרא דהן מנינא ראזהו דאלפא שביעיא · דבה מתנחמין כלהון מיתא ואמרו דזבנא דעלמא לה להוא מנינא תחם ברויה · שבועא גיר תחום איתוהי מפרשנא דזבנא.

This view of the duration of the earth entirely agrees with the familiar Agada in T. B. *Sanhedrin*, 97a:—תנא דבי אליהו ששת אלפים שנה הוי עלמא.

A similar tradition in Jerome is treated by Rahmer:— "*Die hebräischen Traditionen in den Werken des Hieronymos*" (Breslau, 1861), p. 22. A multitude of opinions on *Chiliasm* has also been collected from the Church Fathers and Talmudic doctors by Grünwald, *Verhältniss der Kirchenväter zur talmudischen und midraschischen Literatur* (in Königsberger's *Monatsblätter*, p. 102, also separately printed, Jungbunzlau, 1891).

S. KRAUSS.

(*To be continued.*)

The Jewish Quarterly Review.

JANUARY, 1894.

THE JEWS IN THE WORKS OF THE CHURCH FATHERS.

VI.

JEROME.

THE Latin Father's comprehensive works contain a mass of data concerning the Palestinian Jews, as well as complete accounts of their political, educational, and religious status in the fourth century, which have as yet by no means been exhausted. The following pages give especial prominence to those points which, as far as my view of the literature of the subject extends, have not received adequate treatment. These are, however, so numerous that I have thought it well, for the sake of clearness and conciseness, to divide the subject into sections.

1.—POLITICAL POSITION OF THE JEWS IN PALESTINE DURING THE FOURTH CENTURY.

The Jews seem to have enjoyed the full right of domicile in Palestine and adjacent countries. We find them settled in all parts of the country. Considerable tracts were almost exclusively occupied by them,[1] while Chris-

---

[1] On. Sacr., ed. Lagarde, cxix. 15, 19; cxx. 6; cxli. 27; clvii. 4, etc.

tianity was only spread over that territory which was formerly called Moab.[1] In Judea itself the Christians were only here and there sole occupiers of entire localities.[2] While, however, the Jews were not forbidden by express law to settle in towns and trade centres, they seem of their own accord to have avoided large cities, where their appearance might have occasioned a tumult.[3] For the same reason they abstained from attending crowded markets[4]—so permanent and abiding was the effect of the terrible disasters which they had sustained in their last struggle with the Romans. Under Abraham's terebinth tree, where, as the story ran, thousands of Jewish captives of war had been sold into slavery in the reign of terror that followed the revolt against Hadrian, fairs were held annually and largely frequented.[5] Could the Jews help avoiding a place fraught with such sad memories? For other reasons, too, the commercial cities of the Holy Land were an abomination to the Hebrews. A Talmudic law forbade Jews from entering Ascalon, Gaza, Acco, and Scythopolis, because of their still prevalent idolatry (T. B. *Abodah Zara*, 11b). Cæsarea and Joppa and other towns practised the most shameful rites of heathendom as late as the fifth century.[6] We need not, therefore, wonder that Jerome was impressed by the small number of Jews who visited those cities.

Settlement in Jerusalem, on the other hand, was forbidden by an express enactment, which we learn from Jerome was still in force in the fourth century.[7] They

---

[1] In Is. xvi. 4, In omni terra Moab ecclesia Christi.

[2] On. Sacr. xciii. 18; xiv. 15; cviii. 27.

[3] In *Ep. ad Galat.* iv. 22, Vix rarus atque notabilis in urbibus Judaeus appareat.

[4] In Jerem. xxxi. 14, Idcirco execrabile esse Judaeis mercatum celeberrimum visere.

[5] In Zach. xi. 5, In tabernaculo Abraae . . . ubi nunc per annos . . . . mercatus celeberrimus exercetur.

[6] Neubauer, *Géographie du Talmud*, pp. 68, 232; Schürer, *Geschichte des Jüdischen Volkes im Zeitalter Jesu Christi*, II, p. 11.

[7] In Soph. i. 15, *et passim*.

were hardly permitted to wail on Zion's ruins. This was a privilege which had to be heavily paid for. Jerome dwells with satisfaction on this humiliation.[1] Every year, on the 9th of Ab, wailing and with rent garments, the Jews could be seen traversing the Temple mount, and throwing themselves upon stones pierced with a hole and daubed with oil.[2] They donned mourners' robes, walked barefoot, and rolled themselves in the dust. Even the dish of lentils, usually prepared for those bereaved by death, was not wanting.[3]

In trade and commerce no restrictions seem to have been placed on the Jews. Jewish physicians and innkeepers are mentioned by name in Jerome's works. The former were on friendly terms with the scholars;[4] the latter were accused of mingling their wine with water.[5] State offices were barred to the Jews; so was the military profession. "No wonder," says our author, with malicious satisfaction, "that the Jews have lost their manly bearing. They are not received into the army, nor are they permitted to wear swords or bear other warlike arms."[6]

2.—SOCIAL POSITION OF THE JEWS.

The material condition of the Palestinian Jews must, on the whole, be pronounced favourable. They appear to have been rather rich than poor. Jerome accentuates every species of misery they suffer as proofs that they are no longer God's people; but he has nothing to say of their poverty. On the contrary, it is their wealth which

---

[1] In Soph. Compare Eusebius' account.
[2] Grätz, *Monatsschrift*, 1876, p. 4; Thierry, *St. Jerôme*, I., p. 253.
[3] *Ep.* xxii. *ad Paulam* (ed. Mart. iv. 27), Flent usque hodie Judaei et nudatis pedibus in cinere volutati sacco incubant. Ac ne quid desit superstitioni, ex ritu vanissimo Pharisaeorum primum cibum lentis accipiunt.
[4] Praef. in Osee, in tabernis medicorum, etc.
[5] In Amos ii. 12, Neque possunt more Judaicorum cauponum miscere aquam vino. [6] In Js. iii. 2.

offends him. "Search through all the synagogues of the Jews," he exclaims, "and you will not find a single Rabbi who impresses on his flock the duty of despising earthly possessions, or who praises the virtue of poverty."[1] With biting scoffs he attacks their healthy, practical common sense. They do not pursue chimeras, but toil for the good things of earth.[2] This practical sense shows itself especially in their dealings with Christians. When pious pilgrims engage Jewish guides, they have to pay them heavily for their services.[3] When Christians seek the opinion of Jews in Biblical matters, they have to remunerate them substantially for their instruction.[4] When Christians wish to possess correct copies of the Bible prepared for them by Jews, they must compensate the scribes with considerable sums.[5] When, finally, a Christian, desirous of completing his Biblical education, applies to Jewish teachers, he is charged high fees for the lessons.[6]

This practical cleverness not only obtained for the Jews a good social position. It enabled them also to afford shining proofs of their inborn charitableness, even towards their Christian persecutors. Many a Gentile's wretchedness was alleviated with the money of Jews. But this generosity aroused Jerome's apprehension that the Jews' gold might corrupt the Christian, and convert him to his benefactor's creed. He therefore recommends that Jewish assistance should be firmly and persistently refused.[7] To the honour of the Church be it said that it did not forbid its adherents

---

[1] In Is. iii. 14. [2] In Ez., iv. 13.

[3] In Naum, i. 1; Thierry, a. a. O. I., 236.

[4] Lib. II., *Invect. Ruff.* c. xxix. (II., 658), Judaeus .... verba vendat ad pretium.

[5] Lib. II. *Contra Ruff.* (II., 530), Magno sumptu sibi a Judaeis describere festinavit.

[6] Praef. in Job, memini .... me .... Lyddaeum quendam .... non parvis redemisse nummis.

[7] *Ep.* lii. *ad Nepotianum* (I., 263), Aut aurum repudiemus cum caeteris superstitionibus Judaeorum; aut si aurum placet, placent et Judaei, quos cum auro aut probare nobis necesse est aut damnare.

to give alms to the Jewish poor;[1] although the almoners were only allowed a free hand when the Church members had been particularly liberal.[2] At that time, it was still admitted that God loved the Jews,[3] and that they were not outside the pale of humanity.

3.—INTERNAL ORGANISATION OF THE PALESTINIAN COMMUNITIES.

Concerning the condition of the Jewish communities in the fourth century there are but scanty notices, so that the accounts which Jerome gives us in this connection are doubly welcome.

In early times the government of the communities was vested, not in the religious teachers, but in a few influential heads elected from the laity.[4] This order of things seems to have been changed. Jerome tells us that the religious teachers were the leaders of the community. The spiritual guides were also the secular guardians. In the latter capacity they appear to have been styled *praepositi*. Before assuming office, they had to pass an examination, the object of which was to test their capacity for deciding ritual questions.[5] From one of John Chrysostom's Homilies it is clear that the Jewish Presidents, there called Archontes, were chosen at the beginning of the year, *i.e.*, in the month of September (Loening, *Die Gemeindeverfassung des Urchristenthums*, Halle, 1889, No. I., p. 69). The custom had gradually obtained of "conferring synagogal functions

---

[1] *Ep.* cxx. *ad Hedibiam* (I., 814), Non quod in pauperes Judaeos.... prohibeamus faciendam eleemosynam.

[2] Lib. c. *Vigilantium*, c. xv. (II., 319), Cunctis pauperibus, etiam Judaeis et Samaritanis, si tanta sit largitas, stipe porrigendas.

[3] In Osee iii. 1, Quia Judaei praesens tempus diligentur a Domino.

[4] Schürer, *Gemeindeverfassung der Juden in Rom*, p. 30.

[5] *Ep.* cxxi. *ad Algasiam*, Quaest. X., Praepositos habent synagogis sapientissimos quosque, foedo opere delegatos, ut sanguinem virginis sive menstruatae, mundum vel immundum, si oculis discernere non potuerint gustu probent.

upon those who, searching in the Law of God day and night have no part in earthly benefits, and take God as their sole inheritance. Thus the interests of equity were served. The good things were not unequally distributed; the superfluity of some alleviated the needs of others."[1] Jerome notes a touching instance of Jewish tenderheartedness; Jewish women took it upon themselves to provide religious teachers with their livelihood.[2] Although the communal heads were greatly esteemed by their flocks, their influence outside the Synagogue was not very considerable. Independent jurisdiction had been taken from them. In disputed cases, the Roman magistrates decided. The Jewish authorities were subordinated to them: "They have no judges of their own; even the heads left to them must submit to the decision of the Roman authority."[3] The Patriarchate, the single institution which still shone with some splendour in the dark days of trial, was dying. Nevertheless messengers were still sent out to collect contributions for the Patriarch.[4]

4.—JEWISH FAMILY LIFE.

Jewish family life has always been distinguished by affectionate tenderness. A few noteworthy details may be gleaned from Jerome. Children were sometimes weaned

---

[1] Lib. c. *Vigilantium*, c. xiv. (II. 399), Hac in Judaea usque hodie perseverante consuetudine, non solum apud nos, sed et apud Hebraeos, ut qui in Lege Domini meditantur die ac nocte et partem non habent in terra nisi solum Deum, synagogarum et totius orbis foveantur ministeriis, ex aequalitate dumtaxat, non ut aliis refrigerium, et aliis sit tribulatio, sed ut aliorum abundantia aliorum sustentet inopiam.

[2] Lib. I. *adv. Jovinianum*, c. xxv. [(II., 277), Mulieribus, quae juxta morem Judaicum magistris de sua substantia ministrabant.

[3] In Is. iii. 2.

[4] In *Ep. ad Galatas* i. 1, Usque hodie a Patriarchis Judaeorum Apostolos mitti. Grätz, *Geschichte der Juden*, iv.², 476, only mentions Eusebius and Epiphanius as sources, and omits that interesting remark in Jerome, who even tells the Hebrew name, *Slias* (שליח).

as late as the fifth year.¹ Parents carried their grown-up sons and daughters on their shoulders and in baskets.² In Jerome's time Jews were blessed with large families.³ Of asceticism there was no trace. Within the limits of the law, no check was placed on good living. The meals on Sabbath were excellent. The day was passed in idleness or sleep.⁴

Jerome notes with some mortification that, as a rule, the Jews reached an advanced old age.⁵ A death arouses the sympathy of the entire community. The custom still continued of employing professional wailing women who, with hair uncovered and bared breasts, summoning every one to mourning and weeping.⁶

5.—EDUCATIONAL STATUS OF THE JEWS.

For the education of the young there were elementary schools; and for the adults, Talmudical colleges. Importance was attached to the cultivation of the memory. Children had to learn by heart the alphabet in the regular and reverse order.⁷ The Pharisees are reproached by Jerome with always repeating, never reflecting.⁸ The strength of memory attained by this system of training arouses his admiration and chagrin. "In childhood they acquire the complete vocabulary of their language, and

---

¹ *Quaest. Hebr.* in Gen. xxi. 14.

² In Is. l. 18, Ridiculum est more Judaico grandaevos filios et filias in ulvis humerisque portari.

³ In Is. xlviii. 17, Usque in praesentem diem instar vermiculorum pullulant filios et nepotes.

⁴ In Is. lvi. 2, Neque enim prodest sedere in sabbatho, sive dormire aut epulis inhiare.

⁵ In Is. iii. 2, Usque ad deripiam senectutem saepe venire (Judaeos) conspicimus.

⁶ In Jerem. ix. 17. Cp. Moed Katan, 28b.

⁷ In Jerem. xxv. 26, in ששך.

⁸ *Ep.* cxxvii. *ad Principiam* (I., 947), Meditationem Legis in replicando quae scripta sunt, ut Judaeorum existimant Pharisaei.

learn to recite all the generations from Adam to Zerubbabel with such accuracy and facility, as if they were simply giving their names."[1] It gave them pleasure to annoy the Christians by intoning[2] the long list of grandchildren, great-grandchildren, grandfathers, great-grandfathers, and great-great-grandfathers without a single slip. It was quite a common feat among the Jews to recite by heart the five books of Moses and the Prophets.[3] This strain on the memory was not occasioned by a want of books. It was but an additional proof of the warm love which the Jews cherished for the ancient Law. Jerome often mentions the "Archiva Judaeorum," by which he often merely refers to the Canon of Scripture, but sometimes also means libraries.[4] Jewish houses possessed shelves loaded and cases packed with books.[5] In Palestine, an institution analogous to our circulating libraries must have existed. Every synagogue seems to have possessed a collection of books, from which the members were permitted to borrow. Jerome's Jewish teacher abused his privilege, and presented his Christian pupil with a volume lent him by the Synagogue authorities.[6]

Jerome stood in need of a copy of the Bible which the Synagogue regarded as authentic. Other copies of the Scriptures that were in circulation were most untrustworthy.[7] But even erroneous copies of Holy Writ the

---

[1] In *Ep. ad Titum* iii. 9. The Apostle Paul also alludes to this quality of the Jews. *Ep.* I. *ad Timoth*. i. 4.

[2] *Ib.* putant se in nominibus referendis . . . in nepotibus, abnepotibus, avis, proavis et abavis doctiores.

[3] In Is. lviii. 2. Libros Prophetarum ac Moysi memoriter revolventes (Judaei).

[4] *E.g.* Praefatio in Esther (ix., 1566) librum Esther . . . ego de Archivis Judaeorum relevans.

[5] In Matt. xxiii. 5, Judaei alioquin armariae et arcae habent libros.

[6] *Ep.* xxxvi., *ad Damasum* (i. 158). Subito Hebraeus intervenit, deferens non pauca volumina, quae *de Synagoga quasi lecturus* acceperat et illico habes, inquit, quod postulaveras . . .

[7] *Praef.* in Gen. (ix. 6), emendatiora sunt exemplaria Latina quam Graeca, Graeca quam Hebraea.

The Jews in the Works of the Church Fathers. 233

Christians could not prepare by themselves, their Hebrew knowledge was not sufficiently extensive. They had to order them of Jewish scribes, who charged heavy fees for their trouble.[1] This speaks well for the Biblical knowledge of the Palestinian Jews. Jerome assumes that in Scriptural questions, every Jew, without exception, is competent to give satisfactory replies.[2] The Jews, moreover, were acquainted, not only with the original text but also with the Septuagint,[3] the Apocrypha,[4] Aquila's Version,[5] and generally with all works relating to Holy Writ. No sooner had Apollinaris Laodicenus' writings appeared than the Jews read them and formed their opinions on them.[6] Especially noteworthy is the fact that the Jews were at home in the New Testament as well as in the Old. They could explain difficulties in it which puzzled even the officially appointed Christian teachers.[7] Jerome's Hebrew tutor even quotes Virgil.[8] That this man knew Greek, Latin, Hebrew and Aramaic, is evident from every page of Jerome's works.

6.—RELIGIOUS LIFE OF THE JEWS.

The Synagogue formed the centre of Jewish life. The Jews must have possessed several synagogues, as Jerome

---

[1] *Lib.* ii. c. *Ruffinum* (ii. 530), magno sumptu sibi a Judaeis describere festinavit . . .

[2] *Praef.* in Samuel (ix., 450).

[3] *Ep.* lvii. *ad Pammachium* (i. 234, et passim). The Jews impugn certain passages in the Septuagint.

[4] *Praef.* in Daniel, the history of Susanna is ridiculed by the Jews.

[5] *Ep.* xxxvi. *ad Damasum* (i. 165), Aquilam . . . proprie transtulisse omnis Judaea conclamat.

[6] In Eccles. v. 17, nec Judaeis placere nec Christianis.

[7] In Is. xi. 1, Illud quod in Evangelio . . . omnes quaerunt Ecclesiastici et non inveniunt ubi scriptum sit, eruditi Hebraeorum de hoc loco assumptum putant.

[8] *Praef.* in Daniel (ix. 1362), illud in sua lingua ingerente: Labor omnia vincit improbus.

drops a remark, in his bitter vein, on the number of them.[1] He also knew that services were held in the Synagogue by day and night.[2] He feels surprised that the Jews do not kneel during prayers.[3] Among the Jewish prayers he has much to say concerning the Benediction against the heretics; he also occasionally quotes other Jewish prayers.[4] The most solemn part of the service was undoubtedly the chanting of the Psalms.[5] With especial frequency and solemnity was the 117th Psalm, the Hallel, sung.[6]

Besides prayer and song, the sermon formed an essential part of the Service. Concerning its popularity among the Jews, to which the Midrash bears ample testimony, Jerome also furnishes some data. "They say one to another: Come, let us listen to this or that Rabbi who expounds the divine law, with such marvellous eloquence; then they applaud and make a noise, and gesticulate with their hands."[7] "The Preachers make the people believe that the fictions which they invent are true; and after they have in theatrical fashion called forth applause .... they arrogantly step forward, speak proudly and usurp the authority of rulers."[8] Jerome was an attentive observer;

---

[1] In Is. lvii. 12. Synagogarum turba.

[2] In Jerem. xviii. 17, usque hodie diebus ac noctibus in Synagogis invocant nomen Dei.

[3] In Is. xlvi. 2, genu flectere . . . quod Judaei mentis superbiam demonstrantes, omnino non faciunt.

[4] In Is. lxiv. at the end, there is the following Jewish prayer: Super his omnibus Domine sustinebis et affliges [Var. sustinebimus et afflige] nos atque humiliabis vehementer. I do not understand this.

[5] In Amos v. 23, Judaeorum . . . Psalmi, quos in Synagogis canunt, tumultus (sunt) . . . Domino.

[6] *Ep. xx. ad Damasum* (i. 66).

[7] In Ezek. xxxiii. 33. Venite audiamus illum et illum, mira eloquentia predicationis suae verba volventem; plaususque commovent et vociferantur et jactant manus.

[8] In Ezek. xxxiv. 31. Qui quum populo persuaserint, vera esse quae fingunt, et in theatralem modum plausus concitaverint et clamores, immemores fiunt imperitiae suae et adducto supercilio, libratisque sermonibus, magistrorum sibi assumunt auctoritatem.

the Jewish preacher's theatrical manner is also mentioned by his contemporary, St. John Chrysostom.[1] "On certain days they recite their traditions to their pupils; on such occasions they are wont to say: οἱ σοφοὶ δευτερῶσιν, *i.e.*, 'the masters explain.'"[2] From this last remark we see that Greek terms for purely Jewish institutions had been adopted and were already fixed in popular usage. Thus, the teachers who occupied themselves with Halacha were called in Greek σοφοί;[3] those, on the other hand, who devoted their chief attention to Hagada, were called δευτερωταί.[4] It is remarkable that the title σοφός for Rabbi was maintained throughout the Middle Ages[5] in communities of Greek origin, *e.g.*, in Sicily.

Jerome naturally does not approve of the Rabbinical teachers. He reproves them for not preserving a composed demeanour while preaching, and says they find a pleasure in shouting.[6] Self-maceration—at that time already regarded by the Christians as a virtue—was not practised by the Jewish Rabbis; he therefore regarded them as voluptuaries.[7] He does not believe that these gourmands could bring it upon themselves to fast twice a week, on Monday and Thursday.[8] The nature of a Jewish sermon is also accurately defined. "The Jews," he says, "rush on certain days into the Synagogue and pore in God's law to find

---

[1] *Opp. ed. Montfaucon* (i. 656), καὶ παίξουσι (οἱ νῦν πατριαρχαὶ πὰρ ὑμῖν) καθάπερ ἐν τῇ σκήνῃ.

[2] *Ep.* cxxi. *ad Algasiam, Cp.* שנד חכמים or תנו רבנן.

[3] *Ep.* cxxi. *ad Algasiam* (*Quaest.* x.). Doctores eorum σοφοί, hoc est sapientes, vocantur.

[4] So in several passages.

[5] Gudemann, *Geschichte des Erziehungswesens der Juden in Italien*, p. 289.

[6] In Is. lviii. 3, ad orationem deferatis clamorem.

[7] *E.g.*, in Is. lviii. 3, epulis saturatus Pharisaeus ...

[8] *Ib.* bis in Sabbatho se jejunare jactabant. This seems to be the earliest notice of תענית שני וחמשי, which will correct what Graetz says on the subject in his *Monatsschrift*, 1854, p. 191.

out what Abraham, Isaac, Jacob and the rest of the saints (caeteri sanctorum) may have done."[1] The narrative Agada is here meant, such as we find it in rich exuberance in our Midrashic literature.

The free Agadic homilies at the reading of the Law are to be distinguished from the Sermon. The Biblical verse was first translated, then freely expounded in the Agadic style.[2] The tradition, or Agada, was always connected with a Biblical verse; even a well-known Agada was always repeated whenever a passage was reached in the reading of the Torah with which it had any relation.[3] But not all the Agadas that were in circulation were fit to be publicly read. The recital of several was interdicted[4] on account of their obscenity. Here it should be noted that the Agadas must already have been fixed in writing, as otherwise Jerome could not have spoken of them as being read.

7.—HERETICAL MOVEMENTS AMONG THE JEWS.

Palestine was also in the fourth century an arena, where the various Jewish and Christian sects contended for victory. The *Minim*, who were the objects of so much dread to the Talmudists, were disseminated among all communities of the Orient.[5] There was a multitude of baptised Jews, and the rigorous Talmudic teachers felt

---

[1] In Is. lviii. 2.

[2] In Michaeam ii. 11, juxta id quod nobis ab Hebraeis est traditum exponamus et . . . postea de eorum translatione tractabimus.

[3] *Quaest. Hebr.* In Gen. xiv. 8. Jerome speaks of the Jewish tradition, that the first-born originally served as priests; he afterwards says, Gen. xxvii. 15, Et in hoc tradunt Hebraei . . . The same tradition.

[4] He is speaking of the tradition that Jewish women in Babylon had submitted themselves to certain men of guile, in the hope that they would give birth to the Messiah. (In Jerem. xxix. 21.) Unde et a plerisque ac paene omnibus Hebraeis, ipsa (traditio) quasi fabula non recipitur nec legitur in Synagogis eorum, *Cp.* N. Brüll, Jahrb. iii. 9.

[5] *Ep.* cxii. *ad S. Augustinum*, i. 741, usque hodie per totas Orientis synagogas inter Judaeos haeresis est, quae dicitur Mineorum . . .

called upon to proceed with all possible severity against them; so much so, that the bishops had to intervene in their favour.[1] But these baptised Jews were by no means an acquisition on which the Church could congratulate itself. They either clung firmly to the Jewish enactments, even after baptism, or they led a life which was anything but Christian: "Take any Jew you please who has been converted to Christianity," Jerome writes to St. Augustine, "and you will see that he practises the rite of circumcision on his newborn son, keeps the Sabbath, abstains from forbidden food, and brings a lamb as an offering on the 14th of Nissan."[2]

Transgressions of the Law were not uncommon among the lower classes. Jerome reports that some Jews, on an occasion of mourning, cut incisions in their flesh and made their heads bald.[3] The use of Tephillin and Zizith had not yet become general. Our author is told by Palestinian Jews, as a curiosity, that in Babylon the Rabbis wear phylacteries and zizith.[4] Apostates had to suffer persecutions at the hands of the Rabbis. Excommunications must have been common.[5]

8.—SOME CHRISTIANS STRICTLY ADHERE TO JEWISH CUSTOMS.

Even after more than three centuries' separation, triumphant Christianity had not yet emancipated itself from the mother religion; it was still subject to the influence of the Jewish Law. Our author rails most bitterly at the superstition of the Christian women (*mulierculae*), who, ascribing to the Jewish phylacteries an indefinite

---

[1] Grätz, *Geschichte*, IV. [2] 385.
[2] *Ep.* cxii. *ad S. Augustinum*, I. 744.
[3] In Jerem. xvi. 5.
[4] In Ezek. xxiv. 15; in Matt. xxiii. 5.
[5] In Is. lix. 15, ut quicunque a traditionibus Judaeorum capierit recedere, statim pateret insidiis et persecutionibus, ita ut . . . expulerint de Synagogis.

but vast magical power, covered up crucifixes, the Gospels, and other sacred relics with them, and thought they were thus performing a work pleasing to God.[1] The rites of the Synagogue were imitated;[2] the Christians regarded it, indeed, as holier than the Church.[3] On the occasion of a death they rent their garments after the Jewish custom.[4] About this time arose the order of the Cœnobites, who arranged their mode of life according to the old Essene pattern.[5] At this period, too, the sect of the Photinians was instituted. They adhered so closely to the Jewish Law that their dogma was termed the Jewish dogma, and yet it had to be admitted that there was much in it that was good and wise.[6] It even appears that at that time Jewish birth was considered a weighty factor in the selection of Heads of the Church.[7] But it was mainly the lower classes who could not completely cut themselves off from the Jewish Law, the enactments of which appeared to them more rational and wise than those of Christian codes.[8] The dependence of the Church on the Synagogue is best described by Ruffinus, who sarcastically observes that if a few Jews were to institute new rites, the Church would have to follow suit and immediately adopt them.[9]

---

[1] In Matt. xxiii. 5, Quae habent quidem zelum Dei sed non juxta scientiam. We have come across similar accounts in the earlier Church Fathers.

[2] In Ezech. xxxiii. 33, Tales sunt usque hodie multi in Ecclesiis.

[3] Graetz, *History*, IV.² 385.

[4] This is clear from a notice in Gregory of Nyssa's essay, Περὶ τοῦ βίου τῆς μακαρίας, in Oehler, *Bibliothek der Kirchenväter*, I., 188, p. 2. περιῤῥήξασθαι τὸ ἱμάτιον Μακρίνης.

[5] *Ep.* xxii. *ad Eustochium*, i. 118.

[6] *Chronicon*, VIII., 816, Photiniarum dogma Judaicum, qui [Photinus] multa continentia est ingenii bona uno superbiae malo perdidit.

[7] In Is. lxi. 3, Quotus enim quisque Ecclesiarum princeps est de Judaeis et non de alienigenis atque externarum gentium hominibus?

[8] *Ep.* cxxi. *ad Algasiam*, i. 878, Videntur igitur observationes Judaicae apud imperitos et vilem plebeculam imaginem habere rationis humanaeque sapientiae.

[9] Ruffini, *Invect.*, lib. I., c. v.; II., 589, Nisi forte a Judaeis aliquibus nova nunc lege promulgatur Ecclesiae ut etiam ista discamus.

9.—Controversy between Christians and Jews.

In Jerome's time there was no lack of discussions between Church and Synagogue. The Church militant still enjoyed its youthful vigour; it had both the desire and the strength for fighting. It was considered a great undertaking to enter on a polemic with the Jews.[1] The discussions were conducted with excessive heat; they are described as regular combats.[2] Jerome says that, on the Jewish side, the efforts that were put forth in these verbal contests were appalling.[3] The Jews are charged with an inordinate love of religious disputation. They are in great distress if no opportunity presents itself of slandering and ridiculing the Christians.[4]

With regard to the Jewish method of argument, our author tells us that they never kept to the point, always introduced matters foreign to the discussion, and often wandered away to other subjects altogether.[5] The only construction that can justly be placed on this statement is that the Jews were most reluctant to enter into controversy on certain topics. The same questions also seem to have been put over and over again. The Scriptural text was a perpetual bone of contention, the Jews insisting that the Christian copies of the Bible were erroneous.[6] On some points that had been discussed *ad nauseam* the Christians knew beforehand what their opponents would

---

[1] Praef. in Psalm, Aliud Judaeis singula verba calumniantibus respondere.

[2] In Is. vii. 14, Ut cum Judaeis conferamus pedem . . . . contentioso fune, etc.

[3] In *Ep. ad Titum*, iii. 9, Ut non magnopere pertimescamus supercilium Judaeorum, solutis labiis et obtorta lingua et otridente saliva et rasa fauce gaudentium.

[4] In Is. vii. 14, Nequaquam . . . . . praebeamus eis risum nostrae imperitiae.

[5] In Is. xliv. 6, Judaei . . . . in locis difficilimis liberae disputationis excursu nascentes fugiunt quaestiones.

[6] Very frequently in Jerome's writings.

say.[1] At this time the Jews could claim, among the different sects, many adherents to their principles. Some heretical Christians, for instance, agreed with them on most questions.[2] Influential members of the Church even, who were such important personages that Jerome is afraid to name them, could not help acknowledging that, on some points, the Jews were right.[3] Victorious Christianity had still a formidable opponent in Heathendom, and it was but natural that the Heathens sometimes employed Jewish weapons in their controversy with the Christians.[4] One of the consequences of Julian's attempt to revive Heathendom was a hot attack on Christianity. Julian himself fought it with the pen, and made use of Jewish arguments.[5]

10.—Messianic Hopes of the Jews.

The Church continually cherished the fond delusion that it would ultimately receive the Jews into its bosom. It is noteworthy that, as early as 400 A.D., the Jews were forced to listen to Christian sermons, with the avowed purpose of inducing them to embrace the dominant creed.[6] The daughter-religion was then as much disappointed in her expectations as she has been ever since. Judaism *hoped*,

---

[1] *Ep.* xlii. *ad Principiam*, i. 236, Interrogemus Judaeos, quae sit ista filia (Ps. xlv.) . . . . non dubito, quin synagogam respondeant.

[2] Judaei et nostri Judaizantes—a formula used by Jerome.

[3] In Sophon. iii. 14, Si quis ergo Christinorum et maxime novorum prudentium quorum nomina taceo, ne quemquam laedere videar.

[4] In Matt. xxi. 21, Latrant contra nos Gentilium canes in suis voluminibus.

[5] Compare in Osee xi. 1 ; in Matt. i. 16, ix. 9, *et passim*. It has not yet been sufficiently regarded that the Jews referred many Messianic verses to Julian. We frequently find such interpretations in Jerome.

[6] *Ep.* xciii. *Jerosolomytanae Synodi* (i. 549), Atque utinam sanctorum orationibus non nos inquietarent Judaici serpentes et Samaritanorum incredibilis stultitia . . . . quorum turba quam plurima et *ad veritatem praedicationis omnino auribus obturantes* in similitudinem luporum gregeia Christi circuientes.

and this hope was a tower of strength which saved it from succumbing to the temptations of the Church. The Jews deliberately turned away from the gloomy scenes before them, to revel in the prospect of the brilliant picture which their vivid imagination conjured up. One day the Jewish people will again revive, Israel will become glorious, Israel who is so near to God, Israel who has just cause for pride, and who may confidently challenge the judgment of God and men.[1] Israel's dispersion by the Romans does not involve destruction. God, who was with him by the waters of Egypt, by the streams of Babylon, in the fire of Macedonian persecution, will not leave him when enveloped in the flames kindled by Rome.[2] It is true his numbers are diminished; but still a remnant will always survive at last to witness the arrival of the Messianic era and to experience God's mercy.[3] The outcasts of Judah will be gathered together and brought back to Jerusalem. Great will then be the prosperity of the nation. God will deliver into their hands the sons and daughters of Rome, who will be sold as slaves, not to their neighbours, the Persians and Ethiopians, but to the Sabeans, that most distant of peoples.[4] "Though history has often disappointed them, they endeavour to prove that all the prophecies must ultimately be fulfilled; they transport themselves in imagination to the Messianic times, and console themselves with the reflection that what has not yet come true will be fulfilled in the distant future. Moab,

---

[1] In Is. lviii. 3, Est alia temeritas Judaeorum, quasi fiduciae bonae conscientiae, judicium postulant istum (Ps. xxv. 12) et appropinquare deo desiderant.

[2] In Is. xliii. 2. Thus was this verse interpreted by the Jews.

[3] In Is. xliv. 6, Judaei et nostri Judaizantes dicunt Israel ad modicum derelictum, ut in adventu Christi ejus misereatur Deus.

[4] In Joel ii. 7, Promittunt sibi Judaei immo somniunt, quod in ultimo tempore congreguntur a Domino et reducantur in Jerusalem. Nec hac felicitate contenti, ipsum Deum suis manibus Romanorum filios et filias asserunt traditurum, ut vendant eos Judaei, non Persis et Aethiopibus et caeteris nationibus, quae vicinae sunt, sed Sabaeis, genti longissimae.

and the sons of Ammon, the Egyptians, as well as the Philistines and Idumea, who now afflict the Jews, will then receive their punishment. But why, we ask them, should God punish just these nations? Why not the whole globe on the entire surface of which the Jews wander? Gaul, Britain, Spain, Italy, Africa, in fact, all nations, ought also to be punished for the same offence, for the whole world keeps the Jews in captivity."[1]

It was, indeed, the opinion of the Jews that all the nations who had oppressed them would be called to account. In order that Israel's glory might be complete, the angels will build a new Jerusalem, a beautiful and lofty city, ornamented with precious stones and fine gold.[2] The saints will rise again, re-clothed in their bodily form and re-endowed with their human qualities and capacity for pleasures.[3] The joyous banquets of the Messianic times are painted in the brightest colours. Christians who heard of the delights in store for pious Jews were so attracted by the picture, that they became converts to Judaism.[4] In

---

[1] In Sophon. ii. 8. Making allowances for the exaggeration in the phrase "totus orbis," the above-named countries may, in fact, already have been inhabited by Jews; this passage would thus be the oldest testimony to the presence of Jews in Britain. It is likewise worthy of notice that Jerome only knew this Jewish Agada in its external form. He had no conception that by Moab, Ammon, Edom, etc., the Jews meant, not the extinct peoples, but nations still living. It speaks well for his Jewish teachers that their intimacy with him did not tempt them to betray to him the esoteric significance of the Agada. However, Jerome had enough acuteness to guess that by Edom the Jews really meant Rome: in Is. xi. 11 (רומה, רמה), Semper in Idumaeae nomine Romanos existimant demonstrari.

[2] In Is. xlix. 14, Judaei et nostri Judaizantes putant auream atque gemmatam (Jerusalem) de caelestibus ponendam. As well known, this belief was, in the earliest times, one of the dogmas of Christianity, and served to console its followers for the destruction of the earthly Jerusalem.

[3] *Ruff. Invect.* lib. I., c. v. (II. 589), Est Judaeorum vere de resurrectione talis opinio, quod resurgunt quidem, sed ut carnalibus deliciis et luxuriis caeterisque voluptatibus corporis perfruantur.

[4] In Is. lix. 5, Qui audiens traditiones Judaicas ad escas se mille annorum voluerit praeparare.

their religious ecstasy, the Jews had even definitely fixed the time of Messiah's triumphal entry into the holy city. The new redemption, like the old, will take place in the middle of the month of Nissan, on the first midnight of Passover, as at the Exodus from Egypt.[1] The tradition was also firmly held, that the Messiah would first raise his standard in Babylon, would next march into Egypt and conquer it, and then would finally inaugurate his triumphal entry into Jerusalem.[2] This will, however, be preceded by the war with Gog and Magog, in which much blood will be spilt.[3] Finally, the glorious era of universal peace will set in; in the new and resplendent Jerusalem the Messiah will hold his court, surrounded by all pious nations who will do homage to his supremacy.[4] The Jews will be exclusive possessors of the sacred Scriptures; the Christians who had on account of these writings caused them so much suffering will no longer be allowed to retain copies of the Bible.[5] All disputes and misunderstandings will consequently cease; all nations will cherish the same belief, all will understand and speak Hebrew.[6] Such was the conception then current of the Messianic era.

In connection with the foregoing remarks, it is not uninteresting to inquire what conception the Jews formed of the Messiah's person. It is necessary to note first that the

---

[1] In Matt. xxv. 5, Traditio Judaeorum est Christum media nocte venturum in similitudinem Aegyptii temporis, quando Pascha celebratum est.

[2] In Daniel xii. 6.

[3] In Joel iv. 13, Judaei et nostri Judaizantes arbitrantes ultimo tempore, quando Jerusalem fuerit instaurata, sub mille annorum imperio contra Dei populum esse venturas [gentes Gog et Magog].

[4] In Joel iv. 16, Judaei et nostri Judaizantes putant, Christum habitaturum in Sion et in Jerusalem aurea atque gemmata sanctorum populos congregandos.

[5] In Micha vii. 9, Hoc sibi Judaei usque hodie pollicentur . . . . et ajunt: In die illa . . . . Scripturas sanctas . . . . quae nunc tenentur a nobis tolli de manibus nostris et tradi populo Judaeorum. Compare Exod. Rabba, c. 47, 'כתב לך כו.

[6] In Sophon. iii. 9.

Messiah was called in Judaeo-Hellenic circles ἠλειμμένος, the "Anointed," an exact equivalent of the Hebrew משיח, but that this term must be distinguished from the word χριστός, by which the Christians denominated their Messiah. The name Christ was not pleasant to the Jews, since it had become the watchword of their bitterest enemies, and therefore they preferred to connote the same idea by the expression ἠλειμμένος. That the choice of this word was an open protest against Christianity is proved by Aquila's use of it in the Christological Psalm ii. 2, against which Irenæus made a strong protest.[1] In Jerome's time the word had obtained wide currency among the Jews, and he cannot hide his chagrin at the fact.[2] A Messiah of the tribe of Joseph is nowhere mentioned; the Jews, however, even at that time believed, as we have already noticed, that the Messiah's arrival would be heralded by Elijah.[3] The Messiah's essential nature is defined in the sentence: He will be eternal justice (justitia sempiterna).[4] The Messiah is also the whirlwind and storm that will sweep Israel's enemies off the earth.[5] It is interesting to learn the language which was used in praying to the long looked for Messiah. Here is a petition, clothed in Midrashic form, which, starting from Zechariah ix. 11, 12, quotes several other Hebrew texts. "O Messiah, in whose advent we believe, thou whose dominion will extend to the corners of the earth,[6] in the blood of thy covenant,[7] in which according to Ezekiel (xvi. 6, 22), thou didst find

---

[1] Zipser, in *Ben Chananja*, VI. (1863), p. 181.

[2] We can only quote a few passages; to quote them all would be impossible: Antichristus, ut dicitur, ἠλειμμένος suus, in Is. xxvii. 13; Judaei sub ἠλειμμένῳ suo, in Zach. xiv. 15; Referunt ad ἠλειμμένον, id est Christum *suum*, in Maleachi iii. 1. Compare the following remark.

[3] In Mal. iii., the end, Judaei et Judaizantes haeretici ante ἠλειμμένον *suum* Eliam putant esse venturum.

[4] In Dan. ix. 24, in the name of the Jews, according to Jer. xxxiii. 16.

[5] In Is. iv. 5, Hunc locum Judaei ad Antichristum referunt, quem per turbinem et tempestatem significari aestimant.

[6] ומשלו......עד אפסי ארץ.   [7] בדם בריתך.

Jerusalem, the defiled, and didst plight thy troth unto her (?)[1] in the covenant, which thou didst form with Abraham at the division of the calf, the ram, and the goat; thou didst release thy people Israel from captivity,[2] and from the fiery furnace of the Chaldeans who know no mercy.[3] O Israelites, vanquished (by the Romans), do ye therefore also trust in the Lord; return to the well-fortified city of Jerusalem,[4] for you still have God on your side; God who has promised that like Job you will receive a double recompense for the sufferings you have undergone in exile."[5]

11.—CONCERNING THE HEBREW LANGUAGE.

In the knowledge of Hebrew the Jews possessed an advantage over the Christians that was not to be despised. They were intensely proud of this superiority, and continually annoyed the Christians by letting them feel their ignorance.[6] "The Jews are proud of their knowledge of the Law, and parade the fact that they can correctly repeat by heart all the Scriptural names. As, however, these are foreign to us and we do not know their etymology, we pronounce them faultily. When we happen to make a mistake in the accent and lengthen a short syllable or shorten a long syllable, they laugh at our ignorance, especially if the mistake is in an aspirate or in a guttural. If we do not pronounce these surnames and the language generally— which to us is barbarous—in precisely the same way as

---

[1] Quo compersam Jerusalem juxta Ezechielem in suo sanguine reperisti et inisti.

[2] שלחתי אסיריך מבור.

[3] אין מים בו. A free Agadic interpretation.

[4] שובו לבצרון.

[5] גם היום מגיד משנה אשיב לך.

[6] In Ezech. xxxvii. 12. Solent ridere de nobis et attollere supercilium et inflatis buccis ructare scientiam Scripturarum, si non dicam sensuum discrepantiam, qua si fuerit, jure reprehenditur, si verborum dissonantiam in nostris codicibus potuerint demonstrare. In Is. xxiv. 6, Judaei, qui se solos legem accepisse Domini gloriantur.

the Jews do, they break out into loud laughter and swear that they cannot understand what we say."[1] It must have been very difficult for the Christians to learn the Hebrew language. A friend of Jerome's, the noble Paula, a scion of the Scipio family, was so far successful in the study of Hebrew, that she could intone the Psalms in Hebrew without a trace of the Latin accent.[2] Jerome was still further advanced; he studied Hebrew so zealously, that his Latin, far from influencing his Hebrew pronunciation, was actually modified by it. Even his literary style had become changed by his devotion to Hebrew. At the end of his commentary on Haggai he says: "I entreat you, reader, forgive me for communicating my thoughts without embellishments; do not look in my writings for beauty of expression, I have lost it long ago by my study of the Hebrew language."[3] His works afford ample evidence that this apology was not a mere rhetorical figure. Hebrew idiom is frequent; he employs Biblical turns and phrases, Biblical metaphors and explanations, and continually alludes to Biblical incidents and stories.

12.—THE HEBREW LANGUAGE IN EGYPT.

Of the flourishing condition of the Hebrew language at that period Jerome gives such an astonishing account, that all who have occasion to study the history of the Hebrew

---

[1] In *Ep. ad Titum*, iii. 9, Judaei, qui in eo se jactant et putant Legis habere notitiam, si nomina teneant singulorum ; quae quia barbara sunt et etymologias eorum non novimus, plerumque proferuntur corrupte a nobis. Et si forte erravimus in accentu, in extensione, solent irridere nos imperitiae, maxime in asperationibus et quibusdam cum rasura gulae litteris proferendis. Siegfried who, in Stade's *Zeitschrift für die alttestamentliche Wissenschaft*, 1884, proposed to himself the task of fixing the ancient pronunciation from Jerome's accounts, overlooked this important passage.

[2] *Ep.* cviii. *ad Eustochium*, i. 714, ita ut Psalmas hebraice caneret (Paula) et sermonem absque ulla linguae proprietate personaret.

[3] *Praef. Libri* iii., *Ep. ad Galatas*. He complains, omnem sermonis elegantiam et Latini eloquii venustatem stridoris lectionis Hebraicae sordidatum esse.

tongue are bound to examine it closely. He tells us that, in the year 400 A.D., *i.e.*, about six hundred years after its death in Palestine, its Motherland, Hebrew, as a living language, was still surviving in Egypt. The savants who deny that the ancient Egyptian tongue is a branch of the Semitic stock, cannot refuse to acknowledge that the old Egyptian language possessed Semitic elements in abundance; this they ascribe to the contact, during a period of many centuries, between the Egyptians and the Jews settled amongst them.[1]

Suppose we went a step further and assumed that there remained in Egypt, from early times, a small portion of the Jewish population, who continued to speak Hebrew? It does not need a very lively imagination to accept this hypothesis. It is conceivable that the land which was in a sense, the cradle of Judaism, became its asylum after it had received its first terrible blow, and continued to be its home during the dissolution of the Jewish nationality.

Jerome's account, therefore, ought not in itself to be impugned. It is only a pity that, as generally understood, it does not really exist! Let us examine it more closely. "Everybody knows," he says, "that five towns in Egypt still speak the Canaanitish, *i.e.*, the Syrian language."[2] Now we ask: Is there here any mention of Hebrew? Certainly modern criticism insists that Hebrew is really the old language of Canaan. But Philo terms Hebrew the Chaldaic tongue. In Josephus and the New Testament, the Aramaic vernacular is spoken of as Hebrew, But it is quite inconceivable that Jerome, who knew that Hebrew and Aramaic were totally different and distinct should have confounded the two languages, or even, in a

---

[1] The various views have been collected by E. Meier, in *Die Semiten in ihrem Verhaltniss zu Chamiten und Japhetiten*, p. 70 ff.; and exhaustively treated by Lenormant, *Histoire ancienne de l'Orient*, 9th edition, i. 275 and ii. 46.

[2] In Is. xix. 18, . . . Civitates, quas usque hodie in Aegypto lingua Chanaanitide, hoc est Syra loqui, manifestum est.

critical mood, have hit upon the idea that Hebrew was the old Canaanitish dialect. Why should Jerome have expressed himself in so peculiar a fashion, when in other places he calls Hebrew, scores of times, as it ought to be called — Hebrew? If he referred to Hebrew, why does he say in an explanatory note that he means Syriac? Surely the former language was as well known to his readers as the latter? Does not this note rather prove that a language is here spoken of, whose existence might not have been universally known, and that it was therefore needful to explain the uncommon term—Canaanitish, by one more familiar, Syriac. The Hebrew language, however, could certainly not have been meant. For the present, we will therefore merely assume that Jerome speaks of the Canaanitish tongue. How did he become acquainted with this tongue? He himself explicitly tells us: " I came to Sior, the river of Egypt; . . . to the five towns of Egypt which speak Canaanitish."[1] Thus, we see that, in the course of his travels, he had visited the five cities. The object of his journey was to visit the places named in Scripture; and, therefore, he only mentions those names which there occur, and among them prefers the old to the modern ones.[2]

Here we have the key to the enigma: Jerome uses the old Biblical terms, and calls even the river by its ancient name Sior (שיחור). Consequently, as he expresses himself in Biblical language, he calls the language of Egypt the language of Canaan; and rightly so, for Egypt even then retained its old name Cham.[3] Because Cham, Noah's son, was Canaan's father, the language of Canaan

---

[1] *Ep.* cviii. *ad Eustochium* (xxii. 890, ed. Migne, ser. Lat.), Veniam ad Ægypti fluvium Sior, qui interpretatur *turbidus ;* et quinque Ægypti transeam civitates, quae loquuntur lingua Chanaanitide.

[2] *Ib.* (p. 882) ea tantum loca nominabo, quae Sacris Voluminibus continentur.

[3] *Quaest. Hebr.* in Gen. ix. 18, Usque hodie Ægyptiorum lingua Ham dicitur.

was the language of Egypt (Cham), and in the Bible it alone is mentioned (שפת כנען). Nowhere in the Scriptures do we find (שפת מצרים). Jerome was therefore compelled to speak of the Canaanite and not of the Egyptian language. He never thought of designating Hebrew by the term Canaanite; he indeed says: "The Canaanite language partakes of the characters of Hebrew and Egyptian. It is closely related to Hebrew,"[1] but therefore clearly not identical with Hebrew. What language could this have been? Every reasonable man will at once think of Coptic. When Egypt, or at least Lower Egypt, had become quite hellenised, it was strange to hear Coptic sounds; that this dialect was the vernacular in five towns seemed to Jerome a proof that Isaiah's prophecy had been fulfilled. He was a Christian, and the population of those towns was also Christian. That Coptic was spoken in many other parts of the country did not greatly trouble him, or might possibly have been unknown to him, as he only visited Biblical scenes. Isaiah's prophecy caused him to style this language Canaanitish. And as it was unfamiliar to him,[2] he confounded it with the old Egyptian, *i.e.*, Canaanitish; but finding Semitic elements in this foreign idiom, he could describe it more definitely as Syriac, *i.e.*, related to Hebrew. It is quite time, therefore, that this notice of Jerome should be reduced to its real worth.[3]

13.—JEROME'S JEWISH TRADITIONS.

Jerome has preserved for us a large number of Jewish traditions. In the first place come those which aim at com-

---

[1] In Is. xix. 13, Lingua Chanaanitide quae inter Hebraeam et Ægyptiam media est et Hebreae magna ex parte confinis.

[2] *Lib.* I., *adv. Ruff.* c. 10, Ego, philosophus, rhetor, grammaticus, dialecticus, hebraeus, graecus, latinus, trilinguis, etc.—therefore not Coptic.

[3] Winer *Biblisches Realworterbuch*, II., 500, Anmerk. 1, writes: "Hebrew or Syriac is said to have been transplanted by Colonists (?) into the provinces on the Eastern boundaries of Egypt, and was the vernacular there even in Jerome's times."

pleting the Scriptural story. Jerome usually called these traditions "fabulae," because they are in narrative form;[1] we might term them historical Agadas. In this class he draws a distinction between those legends which lived in the memory of the people, and which he therefore highly valued,[2] and those which were only invented by individuals.[3] The latter class of tradition was either suggested by indications in the Bible,[4] or were the product of pure fancy. Imaginative teachers invented them for the purpose of edification. Jerome was also indebted to his Jewish teachers for the explanation of words and subjects.[5] Verbal exegesis took the form either of grammatical rules,[6] or elucidations of difficult terms; and always, of course, in the spirit of the Agada.[7] The subjects explained are invariably connected with the Bible, and the expositions, with the Jews, rest partly on traditional knowledge,[8] and partly are conjectural and arbitrary deductions.[9] This kind of Jewish teaching is, on the whole, condemned by Jerome. He drew his Jewish traditions and views not only from the oral communica-

---

[1] In Jerem. xxix. 21, he calls the same thing now *traditio*, now *fabulae*. In many places, he uses the expression *fabulae* for the Agada, but then they were always narrative.

[2] *Z. B.* in Is. lvii. 1, concerning the assassination of Isaiah: quod apud eos certissima traditio est.

[3] In Ezech. xlv. 10, Traditionem accepimus Hebraeorum non lege praeceptam, sed magistrorum arbitris inoletam.

[4] In Osee x. 2, tradunt Hebraei fabulam . . . auspicionem suam Scripturarum auctoritate confirmantes.—*Ep.* xxxvi. *ad Damasum*, i. 162, . . . multis Scripturarum locis testimonia contrahentes.—In Daniel vi. 4, hoc illi dixerint, qui propter occasionem unius verbi longas solent fabulas texere.

[5] In Is. xxii. 5, hoc traditionis est Hebraicae et Scriptura non loquitur.

[6] In Is. xl. 9, nec de hac re apud eos ulla dubitatio est, Spiritum sanctum lingua sua appellari genere feminino, Rua codsa (רוחא קדשא).

[7] In Ezech. ix. 3 (קסם) quum ab Hebraeo quaererem quid significaret, respondit mihi Graeco sermone appellari καλαμάριον ab eo quod in illo calami recondantur. The Jew, therefore, spoke Greek.

[8] In Is. xxxii. 14 (עפל ובחן) quas Judaei duas turres in Jerusalem fuisse arbitrantur.

[9] In Is. xliv. 15, Hebraei stulta contentione nituntur asserere.

tions of his teachers and of contemporary Jews, but also from collections of the Midrashim, *i.e.*, from written sources, a point which deserves to be specially emphasised. I have already quoted a passage that some Agadas are not *read* in Synagogue;[1] they must, therefore, have been preserved in a written form. Jerome found, probably in books, Hebrew traditions.[2] He speaks of the secret knowledge possessed by the heads of the Synagogue, which he wishes to reveal to the Latins.[3] He was certainly not told this mystic knowledge, and must, therefore, have copied it from a book. Here I wish to point out another important fact. Jerome translates from the Hebrew into Latin. Although the Jews in Palestine always conversed in Greek, those Agadas were compiled in Hebrew. In Alexandria, however, the Agadas, or rather Apocryphas, were also composed in Greek. Translation usually implies a written original. Jerome must, therefore, no doubt, have seen many Agadas in MS. Yet certain remarks of his point to the fact that he also translated oral traditions.[4] However, whether Jerome had written or oral traditions, it is at all events clear that he translated, and in his versions, as in other translations, the original is still discernible. Accidental agreement between Latin and Hebrew tradition is possible; but when technical terms of the Midrash recur in the Latin, this is not pure coincidence, but a conscious translation from Hebrew. Note the oft-repeated formulas: "Hoc Scriptura nunc dicit = זה שאמר הכתוב; and "Hoc est quod dicitur" = הודא הכריב, which conclude many traditions, when supported

---

[1] In Jerem. xxix. 21, nec *legitur* in synagogis eorum.

[2] In Zach. iv. 2, Haec ab Hebraei dicta reperimus.

[3] *Ib.* vi. 9, Semel proposui arcanae eruditionis Hebraicae et magistrorum synagogae reconditam disciplinam, eam dumtaxat, quae Scripturis sanctis convenit, Latinis auribus prodere.

[4] *Ib.* vi. 1, Haec ut potuimus, immo ut accepimus, nostrae linguae studiosis tradimus. *Ib.* x. 11, Haec ut a Hebraeis nobis tradita sunt nostrae linguae hominibus expressimus.

by quotations from Scripture.[1] The formula, אל תקרי, is called by Jerome, "Non debemus legere,"[2] or "legi potest."[3] He also interprets a word according to the meaning of its parts (נוטריקון = νοταρικόν), but he does not seem to have a special Latin term for it.[4] Many more examples of Jerome's adherence to the wording of the Jewish Agada could be given, but what has been said exhibits sufficiently the undreamed of treasures for Jewish literature that lie concealed in Jerome's works. It is a pity that this treasure has not yet been fully opened up. Attempts, however, have been made. Besides Grätz's essay already noted, there are studies of Jerome's traditions by Rahmer. His writings on this subject are: *Die Hebraischen Traditionen in den Werken des Hieronymos I.; Quaestiones in Genesin* (Breslau, 1861); *Die Hebraischen Traditionen in dem Bibelcommentar des Hieronymos* (Ben Chananya VII., 1864); *Die Hebraischen Traditionen des Hieronymos* (Frankel's *Monatsschrift*, 1866 and 1867). Also in Grätz's *Jubelschrift*, 1887.

While giving a due meed of recognition to Rahmer's efforts, I cannot refrain from remarking that he might

---

[1] In Is. viii. 23, Et hoc—inquiunt (Judaei)—Scriptura nunc dicit. *Quaest. Heb.* in Gen. xi. 28, Et hoc esse quod nunc dicitur. Cp. in Zach. viii. 16; in Sophon. ii. 13, *et passim*. Jerome is so familiar with this formula that he employs it in an Agada which he has been told by Jewish Christians (Is. viii. 23). In a verse from the New Testament (Matt. iii. 17) is another time noticed with this formula (in Chab. iii. 5)!

[2] In Zach. xiv. 20, מצלות, Quod quum a Hebraeo quaererem, quid significaret, ait *non debere nos legere mesuloth sed mesaloth* (var. masalloth) quod significat phaleras equorum et ornatum bellicum. . . . . Similarly b. Pesach 50a (R. Eleazar): כל מצילות שתולנן לסום בין עיניו.

[3] In Nahum iii. 8, Hebraeus qui me in Scripturis erudivit, ita legi posse asseruit: Numquid melior es, quam No, Amon—et ait: Hebraice No dici Alexandriam, Amon autem, multitudinem, sive populus: et esse ordinem lectionis: Numquid melior es ab (*sic*) Alexandria populosa, sive populorum, quae habitat in fluminibus. . . . . Therefore, המון, instead of אמון. Cp. Targum *ad loc.*

[4] In Aggaeum i. 1, זרובבל, Apud Hebraeos ex tribus integris nomen ejus traditur esse compositum: Zo (זה) = iste; rob (רב) = magister sive major; babel (בבל) = Babylon: iste magister de Babylone. The same is found in the Midrash.

have done more justice to the theme. Rahmer does not compare other Church Fathers with Jerome; he even omits to place the parallel expressions side by side, nor does he seem to have any idea that several of these Agadas are already to be found in the so-called Hellenistic literature. The Jewish sources are also treated uncritically. The Jalkut and Midrash Rabba are not enough; the Babli, Jerushalmi, Sifre, Sifra, and Mechilta, finally the Targum, have also some connection with the subject. Here follow a few specimens.

14.—SPECIMENS OF JEROME'S MIDRASHIM.

1. *A Lost Midrash of R. Akiba.*

In Eccles. iv. 13: " Hebraeus meus, cujus saepe facio mentionem, cum Ecclesiasten mecum legeret, haec *Baracibam* (var. Baracchiban, Baracubivan = Rabbi Akiba), quem unum vel maxime admirantur, super praesenti loco tradidisse testatus est.

" Melior est interior homo, qui post quartum decimum pubertatis annum in nobis exoritur, exteriore homine, qui de matris alvo natus est qui nescit recedere a vitio et qui de domo vinctorum, de utero videlicet materno, ad hoc exivit, ut regnaret in vitiis. Quia etiam in potestate sua pauper effectus est, mala omnia perpetrando. Vidi eos, qui in priore homine vixerunt, et cum secundo homine postea versati sunt, eo videlicet, qui pro priore decessore generatus est: intellexique omnes in homine priore peccasse, antequam secundo nascente, duo homines fierent."

This Midrash is interesting, not so much for its contents as for its origin, having been composed by R. Akiba. It is a distorted version of an anonymous Midrash on Eccles. iv. 13, found in Aboth di R. Nathan, Version II., c. 4, p. 30, ed. Schechter, in the Midrash on Psalm ix. 5, in Koheleth Rabba iv. 13, and in Jalkut, Rashi, and other secondary sources. All Jerome's editors have unsuccessfully laboured to find some sense in this passage. It is corrupt simply because Jerome did not understand the Agada which was told him. Of the Jewish sources, the earliest is the Midrash on the Psalms, being the only one composed in Aramaic. Let us compare this source with Jerome's version.

JEROME.	MIDRASH, Psalm ix. 5.
Melior est interior homo qui post quartum decimum . . . . . annum in nobis exoritur exteriore homine.	טוב ילד מסכן וחכם זה צר טוב ..... ולמה צווחין ליה. ילד דהוא מזדווג לבר נש מן תלת עשר שנין ולעילא......זה יצר הרע
Qui de matris alvo natus est.	דהוא מזדווג לבר נש מן טליותיה עד סיבותיה :
Qui nescit recedere a vitio—qui . . . ad hoc exivit, ut regnaret in vitiis.	דכל איברים שמעין ליה ...... ולקרה צוותין ליה מלך דכל איברים שמצין ליה ...... למה צווחין ליה
Qui . . . . pauper effectus est, mala omnia perpetrando.	כסיל דהוא מכוון ברייתא......לארחן בישן :

It is obvious that here we have the original Midrash; but Jerome had not understood it, and makes the best sense he can of it. His further explanations of the passage should be read in conjunction with the Agada he quotes. Moreover, in the Midrash itself there reigns confusion, the cause of which is the attempt to bind together disconnected verses in one interpretation. The passages should be read in the original, and this view will become clear.

2. *An Historical Tradition.*

Quaestiones Hebraicae in Gen. xxii. 21 (בוז). Et ex hujus genere est Balaam ille divinus, ut Hebraei tradunt, qui in libro Job (xxxii. 2) dicitur Eliu, primum vir sanctus et prophetes dei, postea per inobedientiam et desiderium munerum . . . . divini vocabulo nuncupatur (privatur?) diciturque in eodem libro: *et iratus Eliu* . . . . de hujus videlicet radice descendens.

The popular legend that Job, Balaam and Jethro, lived at Pharaoh's court (Sanh. 106ᵃ), brings Balaam into connection with Job. An apocryphal addendum of the Septuagint to the book of Job identifies Job with Jobab, son of Joktan. Various opinions, some similar to and others divergent from the foregoing, are found at the beginning of Bar-Hebraeus' Scholion to Job, printed in Bernstein's Chrestomathia Syriaca (Leipzig, 1832, p. 186). Ibn Ezra regards this legend as Karaitic, originating with יצחק המטקביל (Isaak ben Jasas) whom he ridicules. (See M. Sachs, *Beiträge zur Alterthumskunde II.*, 11 Note.) Jerome knows it also, but not as of Jewish origin; he rejects the apocrypha. But in his view that Elihu and Balaam are identical, he stands quite alone. This isolation sufficiently confirms our view that here, too, Jerome had made a mistake. He seems to have got hold of the Talmudical legend) Sanh. 105^b) that Balaam was descended from Boaz and Ruth; confused by the various traditions, he confounded Boaz (בעז) with Buz (בוז).

3. An Halachic Midrash.

In Ezek. xlv. 13, 14 : Traditionem accepimus Hebraeorum non lege praeceptam, sed magistrorum arbitrio molitam: qui plurimum, quadragesimam partem dabat sacerdotibus, qui minimum, sexagesimam, inter quadragesimam et sexagesimam licebat offerre quodcunque voluissent. Quod igitur in Pentateucho dubium relictum est, hic specialiter definitur propter sacerdotum avaritiam, ne amplius a populo exigant in primitiis deferendis, id es ut sexagesimam partem offerant eorum, quae gignuntur e terra.

Jerome makes a calculation which is either original or part of the tradition received by him, in order to show how this interpretation was derived from the verse in Ezechiel. The Talmudic computation of what constitutes עין יפה, עין רעה and בינוני is also derived from that verse (J. Therumoth VI., 1, 42^d), but it is much less simple (compare Tosafoth, Kidduschim 41^d, *s.v.* תורם). Jerome's calculation seems to be the only correct one. Epiphanius also knew of this enactment. The Pharisees are said to have offered τριακοντάδες τε καὶ πεντηκοντάδες. Compare Hilgenfeld, *Judenthum und Juden-christenthum* (Leipzig, 1886), p. 73.

4. *Seventy Noachide Precepts* (?).

In Zech. xi. 13, Judaei istum locum malitiose interpretantes, triginta argenteos, triginta legis mandata commemorant quae facere jubeantur in lege et rursum triginta sex alia, quae prohibeantur in lege. A remarkable Agada!

Grätz (*Monatsschrift*, 1854, p. 192) refers to T. B. *Chullin*, 92a, where the same verse is explained as enjoining thirty precepts on Noah's descendants. He writes as follows: Jerome has certainly misunderstood the Agada if he thinks it refers to enactments imposed upon the Jews, and speaks of thirty affirmative and thirty or thirty-six negative precepts." It appears to me that we ought first to understand the Agada in its Jewish form before we complain that Jerome recites it incorrectly. Is the reason quite obvious why T. B. *Chullin*, 92a, suddenly speaks of thirty Noachide commandments, whereas usually we know of seven such precepts? It is better to confess with M. Joel (Grätz, *Jubelschrift*, German portion, p. 174) that here we have an insoluble enigma. The riddle will, however, be solved if we take a totally different road to that followed by Grätz in his attempt to elucidate the passage. Among the 613 precepts of Judaism we find in various places that certain of them are grouped together. Thus, besides the division into affirmative and negative precepts, we also find the following classification in *Pesikta di R. Kahana*, p. 51b, Buber:

ר' יוחנן פתח ואכרה לי בחמשה עשר כסף (Hosea iii. 2)
בחמשה הרי חמשה עשר · וחומר שעורים הרי שלשים · ולתך
שעורים הרי ט"ו · הרי ששים · אלו ששים מצות שכתב לנו
משה בתורה ואמר ר' יוחנן בשם ר' שמעון בן יוח' שלוש
פרשיות כתב לנו משה בתורה וכל אחת ואחת יש בה מששים
מצות · ואלו הן פרשת פסחים ופרשת נזיקין ופרשת קדושים ·
ר' לוי בשם ר' שילא דכפר תמרתא אמר משבעים שבעים
מצות · אמר ר' תנחומא ולא פליחי מן דעבד פרשת פסחים

The Jews in the Works of the Church Fathers. 257

שבעים כולל עמה פרשת תפלין · וכן מאן דעבד פרשת נזיקין
כולל עמה פרשת שמטה וכן מאן דעבד פרשת קדושים שבעים
כולל עמה פרשת ערוה :

Much ingenuity has been expended on the interpretation of the division here given, with but dubious results. Moses Tobias, of Hanau, believes it to mean that in *the whole Thora* there are sixty enactments with regard to Passover. This is certainly wrong, as the Midrash speaks of פרשיות, and not of the whole Thora. Heidenheim, in the *Pesach-agada*, enumerates sixty *sections* bearing upon Passover; but this view is opposed to the literal meaning of מצות. These opinions are justly discarded by M. Bloch, in the *Revue des Etudes Juives*, I., 201, who thinks the exact number is not to be pressed, as a round number was given. S. Buber, in his edition of the *Pesikta*, note 163, adopts the view that the Midrash speaks of the number of *verses* contained in the portions relating to Passover. He accordingly endeavours to show that the number, if referring to verses, would work out right. But a close examination reveals the fact that this is not the case. We must also avoid the fallacy of assuming that R. Simon ben Jochai had the same verse division as we have in our Bibles. It is therefore advisable to keep to the literal sense of the Midrash. The Agadists found sixty or seventy precepts, מצות, in the specified sections. Is this number correct? We reply, Yes, though according to our calculation a different number might possibly be obtained. It might be worth while giving in detail the calculation which yields the above number. We refrain from wearying our readers with a dry list of sixty or seventy precepts. However, let us examine ten precepts; if the calculation should prove correct in the smaller, it will probably also be so in the larger number. The פרשת שמטה, it is said, contains ten precepts. The reference here is clearly to Exod. xxiii. 10-19. There we find: (1) חג המצות, (2) שם אלהים אחרים, (3) שבת, (4) שמטה, (5) חג הקציר, (6) חג האסיף, (7) וזג, (8) חגיגה, (9) לא תזבח, (10) בשר בחלב, בכורים.

VOL. VI.   R

We willingly concede that the Agadist's meaning may not have been fully grasped in detail; but it will be seen that, on the whole, the calculation agrees. We have thus gained a sure result: all the precepts, affirmative and negative, are counted which are found anywhere in any section of the Thora.

We now return to Jerome. He says: "Triginta legis mandata quae facere jubeantur in lege." Those words sound like the Midrash: מצות שכתב לנו משה בתורה ...... Further: "Rursum triginta sex alia, quae prohibeantur in lege," which in Hebrew would be rendered וכנגדן כתב לנו ל"ו מצות לא תעשה. Accordingly we must not connect these traditions with the remark in *Chullin*, 92a, as Grätz has done, but with the passage quoted from the *Pesikta*. A group of precepts is discussed as a separate code. If it were permissible to suggest that Jerome was in error when he gave thirty-six as the number of precepts, when really it was only thirty, we could simply compare Jerome's tradition with R. Simon ben Jochai's view; thirty of these sixty precepts would be affirmative and thirty negative. The Scriptural sections in question contain both classes of commandments. The deduction from Zech. xi. 12, 13, would thus also be intelligible. The number thirty appears twice; the phrase ואם לו (ver. 12) would suggest מצות לא תעשה. But if the number thirty-six, and therefore a total of sixty-six is correct, the existence of three traditions may be assumed; one tradition found in that portion sixty precepts, the other seventy, and the third compromised the two and accepted sixty-six as the right number. The characteristic distinction, however, between affirmative and negative precepts shows that Jerome's account gives the original tradition, which is wanting in the Jewish sources, and proves its authenticity, though Grätz is unwilling to acknowledge it. The difficulty, that Jerome speaks of precepts imposed on the *Jews*, whilst the Talmud refers to *Noachide* laws, disappears when we remember that Jerome was thinking of another Midrash altogether. An old Agada is given in the T. J. *Aboda Zara* II., 1, where שלשים כסף are explained to refer to thirty pious men on whom the moral order of the world depends. Diverse Agadas were attached to this verse. Amongst them one told by Jerome might also have been in circulation. As regards the thirty commandments given to the Noachides, we note, first, that this Agada is found in the following passages: B. *Chullin*, 92a; J. *Ab. Zara*, II., 1; *Leo Rabba*, c. 24; Midrash Psalm, II., 5; *Jalkut Exod.*, § 307; *Jalkut Hosea*, § 519. Between these different sources we give the preference to the Jerusalem Talmud, which is distinctly different from the rest. There the following statement is made in the name of מב בר הונא בשם רב: "These are the thirty commandments which the sons of Noah will *one day* take upon themselves" (שעתיד ידין בני נח). The golden Messianic age is here spoken of. The meaning of the Agada thus becomes clear. In olden times the Gentiles were only expected to keep seven commandments; but when the human race will have attained perfection, they will observe thirty. This distinction removes the discrepancy between this Agada and the ordinarily accepted canon of שבע מצות בני נח. To what class do those thirty commandments belong? This is indicated by the T. Jerushalmi, in which תפלין וציצית are mentioned, and by a Midrash on Psalms which gives סוכה ולולב. In this Midrash we read: ננתקה את מוסרותימו אלו שבע מצות שנצטוו בני נח ונשליכה ממנו עברתימו אלו שלשים מצות שהן (Manuscript by Buber) קולעין בהן כגון סוכה ולולב שהן נקראו עבות.

The meaning of קולעין is not quite clear, but the sense is, "These are the thirty commandments which they break." (Cp. B. *Chullin*, 92b, above.) Some positive cause of complaint must have occasioned this remark. We do not think we shall be far out in conjecturing that this passage contained a veiled attack on certain heresies concerning Zizith and Tephillin, Succah and Lulab. Of the former definite accounts are extant; concerning the latter, Succoth and Lulab, only vague suggestions and hints have come down to us. It was a long time before the use of the phylacteries became general. In T. B. *Berachot*, 47*b*, this is said to constitute the difference between *idiotai* (עם הארץ) and scholars (חבר). The latter alone wear Tephillin; the Am-Haaretz does not wish to have anything to do with Tephillin and Zizith.[1] The lament at the neglect of Tephillin is echoed in T. B. *Sabb.*, 130*a*,[2] and resounds in the Rabbinical literature of Spain throughout the Middle Ages.[3] The use of Tephillin was often perverted by superstition, as the Greek name phylacteries already evidences. They were regarded as charms to ward off evils. The Mishna (*Erubim* x. 1) complains that the Tephillin are sometimes used for superstitious and not religious purposes; and we often encounter the expression קמיע = charm, talisman, in connection with Tephillin.[4] Those who did observe the precept seem also to have endowed them with a magical power.[5] According to an old Bòraitha, the women shared this superstition;[6] even Christian ladies, in Jerome's times, made use of Tephillin as charms, as already noticed. So much about Zizith and Tephillin. With Succoth and Lulab something similar must have happened. The difference between the Pharisees and Sadducees with regard to the *Ritual* of the Feast of Tabernacles is known to history. This antagonism may have been revived. The Agada, therefore, which rele-

---

[1] Cp. B. *Sota*, 22*a*; B. *Gitt.* 61*a*; B. *Pesach*, 49*b*, and Rosenthal, *Four Apocryphal Books*, p. 26.

[2] וכל מצוה שלא מסרו ישראל ∙ עצמן עליה⋯⋯כנון תפלין עדין היא מרופה בידם. Cp. *Tosaphoth*.

[3] S. T. J. Reifman, in *Beth-Talmud* II. (1881), p. 52.

[4] Especially in *Masecheth Tephillin*. Kirchbein, *Septem Libri Talmudici*, p. 19.

[5] B. *Erub*, 96*b*, אמר רבא וכי אדם טורח לעשות תפלין כמין קמיע. What Raba in Babylon regarded as improbable might have been the case in Palestine.

[6] B. *Berachoth*, 30*b*, מעשה באישה אחת שהיתה ב' שאת לחבר והיתה קומעת תפלין על ידו where the expression קדמעת must be noticed. Possibly in the Midrash on the Psalm, which we have quoted, we should read קומעין instead of קולעין, "They are superstitious about it."

gates the universal observance of Tephillin, Zizith, Succoth, and Lulab to the *Messianic times* started from the indisputable fact that that consummation had, at all events, not yet been reached. "The Noachides" designates the uncultured populace. It is to be regretted that those commandments have not been written down, so that we are unable to discover the historical background of this remarkable Agada; however, we venture to think that, if not altogether, we have at least partly discovered it. It is to be hoped that an investigator will soon arise who will treat the immense field of the Agada according to the requirements of historical criticism.

S. Krauss.

www.ingramcontent.com/pod-product-compliance
Lightning Source LLC
Chambersburg PA
CBHW020126240426
43673CB00038B/613